formatio

TRADITION. EXPERIENCE.
TRANSFORMATION.

Formatio books from InterVarsity Press follow the rich tradition of the church in the journey of spiritual formation. These books are not merely about being informed, but about being transformed by Christ and conformed to his image. Formatio stands in InterVarsity Press's evangelical publishing tradition by integrating God's Word with spiritual practice and by prompting readers to move from inward change to outward witness. InterVarsity Press uses the chambered nautilus for Formatio, a symbol of spiritual formation because of its continual spiral journey outward as it moves from its center. We believe that each of us is made with a deep desire to be in God's presence. Formatio books help us to fulfill our deepest desires and to become our true selves in light of God's grace.

40 Days with

the Church Fathers

On the

Way

to the

Cross

Edited by

Thomas C. Oden

and Joel C. Elowsky

compiled by Cindy Crosby

An imprint of InterVarsity Press
Downers Grove, Illinois

InterVarsity Press
P.O. Box 1400, Downers Grove, IL 60515-1426
World Wide Web: www.ivpress.com
E-mail: email@ivpress.com

InterVarsity Press® is the book-publishing division of InterVarsity Christian Fellowship/USA®, a movement of students and faculty active on campus at hundreds of universities, colleges and schools of nursing in the United States of America, and a member movement of the International Fellowship of Evangelical Students. For information about local and regional activities, write Public Relations Dept., InterVarsity Christian Fellowship/USA, 6400 Schroeder Rd., P.O. Box 7895, Madison, WI 53707-7895, or visit the IVCF website at <www.intervarsity.org>.

The Scripture quotations quoted herein are from the Revised Standard Version of the Bible, copyright 1946, 1952, 1971 by the Division of Christian Education of the National Council of the Churches of Christ in the U.S.A. Used by permission. All rights reserved.

Cover design: Cindy Kiple
Interior design: Beth Hagenberg
Images: man on deserted path: © Lesley Aggar/Trevillion Images
     isolated door: © Michael Miller/iStockphoto
     wallpaper pattern: © Nikolay Zaburdaev/iStockphoto
     cross of nails: © Jill Fromer/iStockphoto

ISBN 978-0-8308-3567-6

Printed in the United States of America ∞

 InterVarsity Press is committed to protecting the environment and to the responsible use of natural resources. As a member of Green Press Initiative we use recycled paper whenever possible. To learn more about the Green Press Initiative, visit <www.greenpressinitiative. org>.

Library of Congress Cataloging-in-Publication Data

Oden, Thomas C.
  On the way to the cross: 40 days with the church fathers / Thomas
C. Oden and Joel C. Elowsky; compiled by Cindy Crosby.
    p. cm.
  Includes bibliographical references.
  ISBN 978-0-8308-3567-6 (pbk.: alk. paper)
  1. Bible. N.T. John—Devotional literature. 2. Fathers of the
church—Quotations. 3. Episcopal Church. Book of common prayer
(1979). 4. Church year meditations. I. Elowsky, Joel C., 1963- II.
Crosby, Cindy, 1961- III. Title. IV. Title: 40 days with the church
fathers. V. Title: Forty days with the church fathers.
    BS2615.54.O34 2011
    242'.2—dc23

2011023125

P	18	17	16	15	14	13	12	11	10	9	8	7	6	5	4	3	2	1
Y	26	25	24	23	22	21	20	19	18	17	16	15	14	13	12	11		

Contents

INTRODUCTION

✝✝✝

One of the ancient sages of the desert named Abba Agatho said that Satan and the spiritual forces of this world are constantly seeking ways to interrupt a person's prayer life. They know that prayer is one of the only things that hinders them. Other areas of life allow for a measure of rest, but not prayer. This is why St. Paul called on Christians to "pray without ceasing." To pray without ceasing means to develop a heart, mind and attitude that is continually focused on God. We need, in the words of Abba Agatho, to pray "till we breathe out our dying breath. That is the great struggle." Our Lord was engaged in this struggle throughout his ministry as he made his way to the cross that awaited him at Calvary. He knew the importance of a disciplined prayer life.

Each Christian is on the way to the cross in imitation of our Lord, who called for nothing less from each one of us than that we bear our cross and follow him. Each of us must deal with the daily crosses that come our way, as we take up whatever cross has been laid down in front of us. In taking up that cross with the hands of prayer that God has given us, the ancients knew that there was a certain rhythm to prayer that would allow for a deeper engagement with God and his purpose for our lives. This is much deeper than simply allowing our prayer life to be governed by the tyranny of the urgent, or being ruled by whatever is on our minds at the moment. They knew that prayer is not first and foremost about us; it's about the One to whom we pray and his will for our lives.

The early Christians knew this and so they allowed for a structured prayer and devotional life that would allow God to speak to them. They patterned their prayer life after the ancient daily rhythm of baptism found in the Scriptures—the daily dying and rising that characterizes our daily walk with Jesus. We die to sin and rise up to new life in Christ in the power of his Spirit. And yet, we live in a world that is constantly seeking to interrupt that daily rhythm. This daily devotional offers one small resource to help Christians get their spiritual rhythm back on their way to the cross.

How to Navigate This Book

On page 11, you'll find the wording of the daily confession from the Book of Common Prayer. In the daily morning prayer outline (called the "Daily Office"), confession always comes at the start of the order for prayer. It initiates that dying to sin that is essential to our spiritual life. During Lent the confession is also placed at the start of the Sunday order of worship, rather than as a part of the Eucharistic liturgy. Lent is a season of repentance, so if you are reading through this devotional during Lent, you will find that turning to this prayer daily and reading through it will be a worthwhile discipline for reflection in preparation for that rising again that is celebrated at Easter.

The daily reading flow is drawn from a modified and shortened version of the daily morning prayer found in the Book of Common Prayer as follows:

Invocation: Key Scripture verse

Confession: Refer to page 11 for the words of the confession.

Invitatory: Follow the confession with the words of invitation for Lent found on page 11.

Scripture Reading: We have taken the Gospel reading passages found in year one of the Daily Office with some modifications so that we follow Jesus' life through the book of John.

Reflections from the Church Fathers: Excerpts illuminating the passage of Scripture taken from the Ancient Christian Commentary on Scripture.

Closing Prayer: These prayers have been drawn from the writings of the early church fathers and the prayer books of the early church.

Further Reading: A listing of the Psalm texts for the day from the Daily Office. These could be referenced during morning reading or at some other time of the day.

This pattern for prayer will allow you to reflect on your own personal relationship with God, guided by Scripture and the wisdom of those who knew their Scriptures so well. Taking time for such personal reflection was part of what the ancients considered spiritual discipline. Taking the time for such reflection is itself a discipline that provides an opportunity for quiet reflection. "The person who abides in solitude and is quiet is delivered from fighting three battles," Anthony said, "—those of hearing, speech and sight. Then he will have but one battle to fight—the battle of the heart."

Our prayer for you is that as you use this devotional you would be strengthened in your "battle of the heart" to withstand those interruptions from Satan that seek to distract you from your Lord and his plan for your life. May the words of your spiritual forefathers and the prayers that echo their ancient wisdom ground and found you into something deeper than yourself, as they connect you to the saints who have gone before in order to equip you for what lies ahead today and every day.

Joel C. Elowsky

DAILY CONFESSION

Almighty and most merciful Father,

we have erred and strayed from your ways like lost sheep,

we have followed too much the devices and desires of our own hearts,

we have offended against your holy laws,

we have left undone those things which we ought to have done,

and we have done those things which we ought not to have done.

But you, O Lord, have mercy upon us.

Spare those who confess their faults,

restore those who are penitent,

according to your promises declared unto humankind

in Christ Jesus our Lord;

and grant, O most merciful Father, for his sake,

that we may hereafter live a godly, righteous, and sober life,

to the glory of your holy Name. Amen.

INVITATORY

The Lord is full of compassion and mercy:
O come, let us adore him.

BCP RITE ONE

Week One

===

✝✝✝

Almighty God, whose blessed Son was led by the Spirit to be tempted by Satan: Come quickly to help us who are assaulted by many temptations; and, as you know the weaknesses of each of us, let each one find you mighty to save; through Jesus Christ your Son our Lord, who lives and reigns with you and the Holy Spirit, one God, now and for ever. *Amen.* COLLECT FOR THE FIRST SUNDAY IN LENT.

SUNDAY

†

If we say that we have no sin, we deceive ourselves, and the truth is not in us; but if we confess our sins, God is faithful and just to forgive us our sins, and to cleanse us from all unrighteousness. (1 John 1:8-9 BCP)

CONFESSION: See page 11.

SCRIPTURE READING: John 1:1-18

¹In the beginning was the Word, and the Word was with God, and the Word was God. ²He was in the beginning with God; ³all things were made through him, and without him was not anything made that was made. ⁴In him was life, and the life was the light of men. ⁵The light shines in the darkness, and the darkness has not overcome it.

⁶There was a man sent from God, whose name was John. ⁷He came for testimony, to bear witness to the light, that all might believe through him. ⁸He was not the light, but came to bear witness to the light.

⁹The true light that enlightens every man was coming into the world. ¹⁰He was in the world, and the world was made through him, yet the world knew him not. ¹¹He came to his own home, and his own people received him not. ¹²But to all who received him, who believed in his name, he gave power to become children of God; ¹³who were born, not of blood nor of the will of the flesh nor of the will of man, but of God.

¹⁴And the Word became flesh and dwelt among us, full of grace and truth; we have beheld his glory, glory as of the only Son from

the Father. [15](John bore witness to him, and cried, "This was he of whom I said, 'He who comes after me ranks before me, for he was before me.'") [16]And from his fullness have we all received, grace upon grace. [17]For the law was given through Moses; grace and truth came through Jesus Christ. [18]No one has ever seen God; the only Son, who is in the bosom of the Father, he has made him known.

REFLECTIONS FROM THE CHURCH FATHERS

A Blind Person Cannot See the Sun's Light, AUGUSTINE. But perhaps the foolish hearts cannot receive that light because they are so encumbered with sins that they cannot see it. Let them not on that account think that the light is in any way absent, because they are not able to see it. For they, because of their sins, are darkness. . . . For suppose, as in the case of a blind person placed in the sun, the sun is present to him, but he is absent from the sun. This is how every foolish person, every unjust person, every irreligious person is blind in heart. Wisdom is present, but it is present to a blind person and is absent from his eyes; not because it is absent from him but because he is absent from it. What then is he to do? Let him become pure, that he may be able to see God. *Tractates on the Gospel of John 1.19.*

Godhead in the Flesh Seeks to Kill Death That Lurks There, BASIL THE GREAT. Let us strive to comprehend the mystery. The reason God is in the flesh is to kill the death that lurks there. As diseases are cured by medicines assimilated by the body, and as darkness in a house is dispelled by the coming of light, so death, which held sway over human nature, is done away with by the coming of God. And as ice formed on water covers its surface as long as night and darkness last but melts under the warmth of the sun, so death reigned until the coming of Christ; but when the grace of God our Savior appeared and the Sun of justice rose, death was swallowed up in victory, unable to bear the presence of true life. How great is God's goodness, how deep his love for us! *Homily on Christ's Ancestry 2.6.*

CLOSING PRAYER

Almighty God, Who sees that we have no power of ourselves to help ourselves; keep us both outwardly in our bodies, and inwardly in our souls; that we may be defended from all adversities which may happen to the body, and from all evil thoughts which may assault and hurt the soul; through Jesus Christ our Lord. Amen. *Gregorian Sacramentary*

FURTHER READING: Psalm 63:1-8; 98; 103

MONDAY

✝

If we say that we have no sin, we deceive ourselves, and the truth is not in us; but if we confess our sins, God is faithful and just to forgive us our sins, and to cleanse us from all unrighteousness. (1 John 1:8-9 BCP)

CONFESSION: See page 11.

SCRIPTURE READING: John 1:29-34

[29]The next day he saw Jesus coming toward him, and said, "Behold, the Lamb of God, who takes away the sin of the world! [30]This is he of whom I said, 'After me comes a man who ranks before me, for he was before me.' [31]I myself did not know him; but for this I

came baptizing with water, that he might be revealed to Israel." [32]And John bore witness, "I saw the Spirit descend as a dove from heaven, and it remained on him. [33]I myself did not know him; but he who sent me to baptize with water said to me, 'He on whom you see the Spirit descend and remain, this is he who baptizes with the Holy Spirit.' [34]And I have seen and have borne witness that this is the Son of God."

REFLECTIONS FROM THE CHURCH FATHERS

John's Preparatory Task, CYRIL OF ALEXANDRIA. No longer does John need to "prepare the way," since the one for whom the preparation was being made is right there before his eyes. . . . But now he who of old was dimly pictured, the very Lamb, the spotless Sacrifice, is led to the slaughter for all, that he might drive away the sin of the world, that he might overturn the destroyer of the earth, that dying for all he might annihilate death, that he might undo the curse that is upon us. . . . For one Lamb died for all, saving the whole flock on earth to God the Father, one for all, that he might subject all to God. *Commentary on the Gospel of John 2.1.*

Why Jesus Was Baptized, CHRYSOSTOM. Jesus then did not need baptism, nor did that washing have any other object than to prepare for all others a way to faith in Christ. For [the Baptist] did not say, "that I might cleanse those who are baptized" or "that I might deliver them from their sins" but "that he should be made known to Israel." And why, tell me, could he not have preached without baptism and still brought the multitudes to him? But this would not have made it any easier. For they would not have all run together like they did, if the preaching had been without baptism. They would not by the comparison have learned his superiority. The multitude came together not to hear his words, but for what? They came to be "baptized, confessing their sins." But when they came, they were taught the matters pertaining to Christ and the difference of his baptism. Yet even this baptism of John was of greater dignity than the Jewish one, and therefore all ran to it; yet even so it was imperfect. *Homilies on the Gospel of John 17.2.*

CLOSING PRAYER

O God, forasmuch as our strength is in you, mercifully grant that your Holy Spirit may in all things direct and rule our hearts; through Jesus Christ our Lord. Amen. *Gelasian Sacramentary*

FURTHER READING: Psalm 41; 44; 52

TUESDAY

†

If we say that we have no sin, we deceive ourselves, and the truth is not in us; but if we confess our sins, God is faithful and just to forgive us our sins, and to cleanse us from all unrighteousness. (1 John 1:8-9 BCP)

CONFESSION: See page 11.

SCRIPTURE READING: John 2:1-12

[1]On the third day there was a marriage at Cana in Galilee, and the mother of Jesus was there; [2]Jesus also was invited to the marriage, with his disciples. [3]When the wine failed, the mother of Jesus said to him, "They have no wine." [4]And Jesus said to her, "O woman, what have you to do with me? My hour has not yet come." [5]His mother said to the servants, "Do whatever he tells you." [6]Now six stone jars were standing there, for the Jewish rites of purification,

each holding twenty or thirty gallons. [7]Jesus said to them, "Fill the jars with water." And they filled them up to the brim. [8]He said to them, "Now draw some out, and take it to the steward of the feast." So they took it. [9]When the steward of the feast tasted the water now become wine, and did not know where it came from (though the servants who had drawn the water knew), the steward of the feast called the bridegroom [10]and said to him, "Every man serves the good wine first; and when men have drunk freely, then the poor wine; but you have kept the good wine until now." [11]This, the first of his signs, Jesus did at Cana in Galilee, and manifested his glory; and his disciples believed in him.

[12]After this he went down to Capernaum, with his mother and his brothers and his disciples; and there they stayed for a few days.

Reflections from the Church Fathers

Jesus Knows to Wait for the Hour Foreknown by the Father, IRE-NAEUS. With [Jesus], nothing is incomplete or done at the wrong time, just as with the Father there is nothing haphazard. The Lord checked Mary's untimely haste when she was urging him to perform the wonderful miracle of the wine and wanting him to partake of the cup, which would have so much emblematic significance later on. This is why he said, "Woman, what have I to do with you? My hour is not yet come"—waiting for the hour that was foreknown by the Father. *Against Heresies 3.16.7.*

The Miracle Continues at the Church's Banquet, ROMANUS MELODUS. When Christ, as a sign of His power, clearly changed the water into wine
All the crowd rejoiced, for they considered the taste marvelous.
Now we all partake at the banquet in the church
For Christ's blood is changed into wine
And we drink it with holy joy,
Praising the great bridegroom,

For he is the true bridegroom, the Son of Mary,
The Word before all time who took the form of a servant,
He who has in wisdom created all things.
Kontakion on the Marriage at Cana 7.20.

Closing Prayer

Almighty God, give us wisdom to perceive you, intellect to understand you, diligence to seek you, patience to wait for you, eyes to
behold you, a heart to meditate upon you and life to proclaim you,
through the power of the Spirit of our Lord Jesus Christ. *Attributed to St. Benedict*

Further Reading: Psalm 45; 47; 48

Wednesday

If we say that we have no sin, we deceive ourselves, and the truth
is not in us; but if we confess our sins, God is faithful and just
to forgive us our sins, and to cleanse us from all unrighteousness.
(1 John 1:8-9 BCP)

Confession: See page 11.

Scripture Reading: John 2:13-22

[13]The Passover of the Jews was at hand, and Jesus went up to Jerusalem. [14]In the temple he found those who were selling oxen and
sheep and pigeons, and the money-changers at their business. [15]And
making a whip of cords, he drove them all, with the sheep and oxen,

out of the temple; and he poured out the coins of the money-changers and overturned their tables. [16]And he told those who sold the pigeons, "Take these things away; you shall not make my Father's house a house of trade." [17]His disciples remembered that it was written, "Zeal for thy house will consume me." [18]The Jews then said to him, "What sign have you to show us for doing this?" [19]Jesus answered them, "Destroy this temple, and in three days I will raise it up." [20]The Jews then said, "It has taken forty-six years to build this temple, and will you raise it up in three days?" [21]But he spoke of the temple of his body. [22]When therefore he was raised from the dead, his disciples remembered that he had said this; and they believed the scripture and the word which Jesus had spoken.

Reflections from the Church Fathers

Selling the Holy Spirit, Augustine. Nevertheless, in order to seek the mystery of the deed in the figurative meaning, who are they who sell the oxen? Who are they who sell the sheep and doves? They are those who seek their own interests in the church rather than those of Jesus Christ. Those who have no desire for redemption have everything for sale. They do not want to be bought; they want to sell. Yet surely it is for their good that they be redeemed by the blood of Christ so that they may attain the peace of Christ. For what profit is there in acquiring anything temporal or transitory in this world—whether it be money, or gorging oneself on food or achieving high honors from your fellow human beings? Are not all things smoke and wind? Do not all things pass on in a moment? And woe to those who want to hang on to passing things, for they pass with them! *Tractates on the Gospel of John 10.6.1-3.*

Our Souls Are the Temple of Christ, Origen. Now Christ is especially jealous for the house of God in each of us, not wishing it to be a house of merchandise or that the house of prayer become a den of thieves, since he is the son of a jealous God. . . . [These words] set forth the fact that God wishes nothing alien to his will to be mingled with the soul of anyone, but especially with the soul of those who wish to receive [the teachings of the] most divine faith. *Commentary on the Gospel of John 10.221.*

CLOSING PRAYER

We implore you, Almighty God, let our souls enjoy this their desire, to be enkindled by your Spirit, that being filled, as lamps, by the Divine gift, we may shine like blazing lights before the Presence of your Son Christ at His coming; through the same Jesus Christ our Lord. Amen. *Gelasian Sacramentary*

FURTHER READING: Psalm 49; 53; 119:49-72

THURSDAY

†

If we say that we have no sin, we deceive ourselves, and the truth is not in us; but if we confess our sins, God is faithful and just to forgive us our sins, and to cleanse us from all unrighteousness. (1 John 1:8-9 BCP)

CONFESSION: See page 11.

SCRIPTURE READING: John 2:23–3:15

[23]Now when he was in Jerusalem at the Passover feast, many believed in his name when they saw the signs which he did; [24]but Jesus did not trust himself to them, [25]because he knew all men and needed no one to bear witness of man; for he himself knew what was in man.

John 3

[1]Now there was a man of the Pharisees, named Nicodemus, a ruler of the Jews. [2]This man came to Jesus by night and said to him, "Rabbi, we know that you are a teacher come from God; for no one can do these signs that you do, unless God is with him." [3]Jesus answered him, "Truly, truly, I say to you, unless one is born anew, he cannot see the kingdom of God." [4]Nicodemus said to him, "How can a man be born when he is old? Can he enter a second time into his mother's womb and be born?" [5]Jesus answered, "Truly, truly, I say to you, unless one is born of water and the Spirit, he cannot enter the kingdom of God. [6]That which is born of the flesh is flesh, and that which is born of the Spirit is spirit. [7]Do not marvel that I said to you, 'You must be born anew.' [8]The wind blows where it wills, and you hear the sound of it, but you do not know whence it comes or whither it goes; so it is with every one who is born of the Spirit." [9]Nicodemus said to him, "How can this be?" [10]Jesus answered him, "Are you a teacher of Israel, and yet you do not understand this? [11]Truly, truly, I say to you, we speak of what we know, and bear witness to what we have seen; but you do not receive our testimony. [12]If I have told you earthly things and you do not believe, how can you believe if I tell you heavenly things? [13]No one has ascended into heaven but he who descended from heaven, the Son of man. [14]And as Moses lifted up the serpent in the wilderness, so must the Son of man be lifted up, [15]that whoever believes in him may have eternal life."

REFLECTIONS FROM THE CHURCH FATHERS

Decaying Flesh Born Again, LEO THE GREAT. Whoever of you, therefore, takes pride (with devotion and faith) in the name of Christian, ponder, by an accurate judgment, the grace of this reconciliation. To you once "cast aside," to you driven out from the thrones of "paradise," to you dying from long exiles, to you scattered into "dust" and ashes, who had no longer any hope of living—to you has "power" been given through the incarnation of the Word. With it, you can "return from far away" to your Maker, can recognize your Father, can become free from slavery and can be made again a child rather than an outsider. With this power, you who were born of flesh that is subject to decay can be "born again from the Spirit" of God and can obtain through grace what you do not have through nature. *Sermon 22.5.1.*

The Story of Moses and the Brass Serpent, CYRIL OF ALEXANDRIA. This story is a type of the whole mystery of the incarnation. For the serpent signifies bitter and deadly sin, which was devouring the whole race on the earth . . . biting the Soul of man and infusing it with the venom of wickedness. And there is no way that we could have escaped being conquered by it, except by the relief that comes only from heaven. The Word of God then was made in the likeness of sinful flesh, "that he might condemn sin in the flesh," as it is written. In this way, he becomes the Giver of unending salvation to those who comprehend the divine doctrines and gaze on him with steadfast faith. But the serpent, being fixed upon a lofty base, signifies that Christ was clearly manifested by his passion on the cross, so that none could fail to see him. *Commentary on the Gospel of John 2.1.*

CLOSING PRAYER

O Lamb of God, who takes away the sin of the world, look upon us and have mercy upon us; you who are yourself both victim and Priest, yourself both Reward and Redeemer, keep safe from evil all those whom you have redeemed, O Savior of the world. *Irenaeus of Lyons*

FURTHER READING: Psalm 19; 46; 50; 59; 60

FRIDAY

✝

If we say that we have no sin, we deceive ourselves, and the truth is not in us; but if we confess our sins, God is faithful and just to forgive us our sins, and to cleanse us from all unrighteousness. (1 John 1:8-9 BCP)

CONFESSION

The Lord is full of compassion and mercy: O come, let us adore him.

SCRIPTURE READING: John 3:16-21

[16]For God so loved the world that he gave his only Son, that whoever believes in him should not perish but have eternal life. [17]For God sent the Son into the world, not to condemn the world, but that the world might be saved through him. [18]He who believes in him is not condemned; he who does not believe is condemned already, because he has not believed in the name of the only Son of God. [19]And this is the judgment, that the light has come into the world, and men loved darkness rather than light, because their deeds were evil. [20]For every one who does evil hates the light, and does not come to the light, lest his deeds should be exposed. [21]But he who does what is true comes to the light, that it may be clearly seen that his deeds have been wrought in God.

REFLECTIONS FROM THE CHURCH FATHERS

Christ the Life of the World, AUGUSTINE. Unless the Father, you see, had handed over life, we would not have had life. And unless life itself had died, death would not have been slain. It is the Lord Christ himself, of course, that is life, about whom John the Evangelist says, "This is the true God and eternal life." It was he himself that through the prophet had also threatened death with death, saying, "I will be your death, O death; I will be your sting." This was as though he had said, "I will slay you by dying. I will swallow you up. I will take all your power away from you. I will rescue the captives you have held. You wanted to hold me, though innocent. It is right that you should lose those you had the power to hold." *Sermon 265b.4.*

The Good Rejoices in Being Seen, TERTULLIAN. The things that make us luminaries of the world are these—our good works. What is good, moreover (provided it is true and full), does not love darkness: it rejoices in being seen and exults over the very recognition it receives. To Christian modesty it is not enough to be so but to also appear so. For its fullness should be so great that it flows out from the mind to the clothing and bursts out from the conscience to the outward appearance. *On the Dress of Women 2.13.*

CLOSING PRAYER

Eternal God, the refuge of all your children, in our weakness you are our strength, in our darkness our light, in our sorrow our comfort and peace. May we always live in your presence, and serve you in our daily lives; through Jesus Christ our Lord. *Boniface*

FURTHER READING: Psalm 40; 51; 54; 95

SATURDAY

†

If we say that we have no sin, we deceive ourselves, and the truth is not in us; but if we confess our sins, God is faithful and just to forgive us our sins, and to cleanse us from all unrighteousness. (1 John 1:8-9 BCP)

CONFESSION: See page 11.

SCRIPTURE READING: John 3:22-36

²²After this Jesus and his disciples went into the land of Judea; there he remained with them and baptized. ²³John also was baptizing at Aenon near Salim, because there was much water there; and people came and were baptized. ²⁴For John had not yet been put in prison.

²⁵Now a discussion arose between John's disciples and a Jew over purifying. ²⁶And they came to John, and said to him, "Rabbi, he who was with you beyond the Jordan, to whom you bore witness, here he is, baptizing, and all are going to him." ²⁷John answered, "No one can receive anything except what is given him from heaven. ²⁸You yourselves bear me witness, that I said, I am not the Christ, but I have been sent before him. ²⁹He who has the bride is the bridegroom; the friend of the bridegroom, who stands and hears him, rejoices greatly at the bridegroom's voice; therefore this joy of mine is now full. ³⁰He must increase, but I must decrease."

³¹He who comes from above is above all; he who is of the earth belongs to the earth, and of the earth he speaks; he who comes from heaven is above all. ³²He bears witness to what he has seen and heard, yet no one receives his testimony; ³³he who receives his testimony sets his seal to this, that God is true. ³⁴For he whom

God has sent utters the words of God, for it is not by measure that
he gives the Spirit; [35]the Father loves the Son, and has given all
things into his hand. [36]He who believes in the Son has eternal life;
he who does not obey the Son shall not see life, but the wrath of
God rests upon him.

REFLECTIONS FROM THE CHURCH FATHERS

Jesus Not Afraid to Go to Judea, CHRYSOSTOM. Nothing can be
clearer or bolder than truth. . . . It neither seeks concealment nor
avoids danger, it fears no plots or cares for popularity. It is subject
to no human weakness. . . . Our Lord went up to Jerusalem at the
feasts to teach the people and help them through his miracles.
After the festival he often visited the crowds who were gathered at
the Jordan, choosing the most crowded places, not ostentatiously
or out of love of honor but because he wanted to help the greatest
number of people. *Homilies on the Gospel of John 29.1.*

What Do You Have That You Did Not Receive? CYRIL OF ALEXAN-
DRIA. He says that there is nothing good in humankind, but everything is a gift of God. It is therefore fitting for the creation to hear,
"What do you have that you did not receive?" I think then that we
ought to be content with the measures allotted to us and to rejoice
in the honors assigned to us from heaven. But, by no means,
should we stretch out beyond what has been given us, nor in our
desire of things greater, appear to be unthankful or to despise the
decree from above and fight against the judgment of the Lord. . . .
Whatever God shall deign to honor us with, [let us] value that
highly. *Commentary on the Gospel of John 2.1.*

CLOSING PRAYER

I know, O Lord, and do with all humility acknowledge myself an
object altogether unworthy of your love; but I am sure that you are
an object altogether worthy of mine. I am not good enough to

serve you, but you have a right to the best service I can pay. Do impart then to me some of that excellence, and that shall supply my own lack of worth. Help me to stop sinning, according to your will, that I may be capable of serving you according to my duty. Enable me so to guard and govern myself, so to begin and finish my course that, when the race of life is run, I may sleep in peace and rest in you. Be with me unto the end, that my sleep may be rest indeed, my rest perfect security, and that security a blessed eternity. *Augustine*

FURTHER READING: Psalm 55; 138; 139:1-23

Week Two

O God, whose glory it is always to have mercy: Be gracious to all who have gone astray from your ways, and bring them again with penitent hearts and steadfast faith to embrace and hold fast the unchangeable truth of thy Word, Jesus Christ your Son; who with you and the Holy Spirit lives and reigns, one God, for ever and ever. *Amen.*
COLLECT FOR THE SECOND SUNDAY IN LENT.

Sunday

†

Rend your heart, and not your garments, and return to the Lord your God, for he is gracious and merciful, slow to anger and abounding in steadfast love, and repents of evil. (Joel 2:13 BCP)

Confession: See page 11.

Scripture Reading: John 4:1-26

[1]Now when the Lord knew that the Pharisees had heard that Jesus was making and baptizing more disciples than John [2](although Jesus himself did not baptize, but only his disciples), [3]he left Judea and departed again to Galilee. [4]He had to pass through Samaria. [5]So he came to a city of Samaria, called Sychar, near the field that Jacob gave to his son Joseph. [6]Jacob's well was there, and so Jesus, wearied as he was with his journey, sat down beside the well. It was about the sixth hour.

[7]There came a woman of Samaria to draw water. Jesus said to her, "Give me a drink." [8]For his disciples had gone away into the city to buy food. [9]The Samaritan woman said to him, "How is it that you, a Jew, ask a drink of me, a woman of Samaria?" For Jews have no dealings with Samaritans. [10]Jesus answered her, "If you knew the gift of God, and who it is that is saying to you, 'Give me a drink,' you would have asked him, and he would have given you living water." [11]The woman said to him, "Sir, you have nothing to draw with, and the well is deep; where do you get that living water? [12]Are you greater than our father Jacob, who gave us the well, and drank from it himself, and his sons, and his cattle?" [13]Jesus said to her, "Every one who drinks of this water will thirst again, [14]but whoever drinks of the water that I shall give him will never thirst;

the water that I shall give him will become in him a spring of water welling up to eternal life." [15]The woman said to him, "Sir, give me this water, that I may not thirst, nor come here to draw."

[16]Jesus said to her, "Go, call your husband, and come here." [17]The woman answered him, "I have no husband." Jesus said to her, "You are right in saying, 'I have no husband'; [18]for you have had five husbands, and he whom you now have is not your husband; this you said truly." [19]The woman said to him, "Sir, I perceive that you are a prophet. [20]Our fathers worshiped on this mountain; and you say that in Jerusalem is the place where men ought to worship." [21]Jesus said to her, "Woman, believe me, the hour is coming when neither on this mountain nor in Jerusalem will you worship the Father. [22]You worship what you do not know; we worship what we know, for salvation is from the Jews. [23]But the hour is coming, and now is, when the true worshipers will worship the Father in spirit and truth, for such the Father seeks to worship him. [24]God is spirit, and those who worship him must worship in spirit and truth." [25]The woman said to him, "I know that Messiah is coming (he who is called Christ); when he comes, he will show us all things." [26]Jesus said to her, "I who speak to you am he."

REFLECTIONS FROM THE CHURCH FATHERS

Human Nature Buds into a Virtuous Life, CYRIL OF ALEXANDRIA. Jesus calls the quickening gift of the Spirit "living water" because mere human nature is parched to its very roots, now rendered dry and barren of all virtue by the crimes of the devil. But now human nature runs back to its pristine beauty, and drinking in that which is life-giving, it is made beautiful with a variety of good things and, budding into a virtuous life, it sends out healthy shoots of love toward God. *Commentary on the Gospel of John 2.4.*

Spiritual Prayer, ABRAHAM OF NATHPAR. Do not imagine, my beloved, that prayer consists solely of words or that it can be learned by means of words. No, listen to the truth of the matter from our Lord: spiritual prayer is not learned and does not reach fullness as a result of either learning or the repetition of words. For it is not to a man that you are praying, before whom you can repeat a well-composed speech. It is to him who is Spirit that you are directing the movements of prayer. You should pray, therefore, in spirit, seeing that he is spirit. He shows that no special place or vocal utterance is required for someone who prays in fullness to God. *On Prayer and Silence 1-2.*

CLOSING PRAYER

I beseech you, merciful God, to allow me to drink from the stream which flows from your fountain of life. May I taste the sweet beauty of its waters, which sprang from the very depths of your truth. O Lord, you are that fountain from which I desire with all my heart to drink. Give me, Lord Jesus, this water, that it may quench the burning spiritual thirst within my soul, and purify me from all sin. I know, King of Glory, that I am asking from you a great gift. But you give to your faithful people without counting the cost, and you promise even greater things in the future. Indeed, nothing is greater than yourself, and you have given yourself to mankind on the cross. Therefore, in praying for the waters of life, I am praying that you, the source of those waters, will give yourself to me. You are my light, my salvation, my food, my drink, my God. *Columbanus*

FURTHER READING: Psalm 8; 24; 29; 84

Monday

✝

Rend your heart, and not your garments, and return to the Lord your God, for he is gracious and merciful, slow to anger and abounding in steadfast love, and repents of evil. (Joel 2:13 BCP)

CONFESSION: See page 11.

SCRIPTURE READING: John 4:27-42

[27]Just then his disciples came. They marveled that he was talking with a woman, but none said, "What do you wish?" or, "Why are you talking with her?" [28]So the woman left her water jar, and went away into the city, and said to the people, [29]"Come, see a man who told me all that I ever did. Can this be the Christ?" [30]They went out of the city and were coming to him.

[31]Meanwhile the disciples besought him, saying, "Rabbi, eat." [32]But he said to them, "I have food to eat of which you do not know." [33]So the disciples said to one another, "Has any one brought him food?" [34]Jesus said to them, "My food is to do the will of him who sent me, and to accomplish his work. [35]Do you not say, 'There are yet four months, then comes the harvest'? I tell you, lift up your eyes, and see how the fields are already white for harvest. [36]He who reaps receives wages, and gathers fruit for eternal life, so that sower and reaper may rejoice together. [37]For here the saying holds true, 'One sows and another reaps.' [38]I sent you to reap that for which you did not labor; others have labored, and you have entered into their labor."

[39]Many Samaritans from that city believed in him because of the woman's testimony, "He told me all that I ever did." [40]So when the Samaritans came to him, they asked him to stay with them; and he

stayed there two days. [41]And many more believed because of his word. [42]They said to the woman, "It is no longer because of your words that we believe, for we have heard for ourselves, and we know that this is indeed the Savior of the world."

REFLECTIONS FROM THE CHURCH FATHERS

The Woman Leaves Carrying Other Water, ROMANUS MELODUS.
But when the Merciful One was near the spring, . . .
Then the woman of Samaria, coming from her native
    village, Sichar, arrived, and she had her urn on her shoulders;
And who would not call blessed the arrival and departure of this
    woman?
For she departed in filth; she entered into the figure of the
    church as blameless;
She departed, and she drew out life like a sponge.
She departed bearing water; she became a bearer of God;
And who does not bless
This woman; or rather who does not revere her, the type of the
    nations
As she brings
Exceeding great joy and redemption?
Kontakion on the Woman of Samaria 9.5.

Lift Up Your Eyes, ORIGEN. "Lift up your eyes" occurs in many places in Scripture when the divine Word admonishes us to exalt and lift up our thoughts, and to elevate the insight that lies below in a rather sickly condition and is stooped and completely incapable of looking up, as is written for instance in Isaiah, "lift up your eyes on high and see. Who has made all these things known?" . . . No one who indulges his passions and clings to the flesh with a concern for material things has observed the command that says, "Lift up your eyes." Such a person will not see the fields, even if they are "already white for harvest." *Commentary on the Gospel of John 13.274, 278.*

CLOSING PRAYER

Let us take refuge like deer beside the fountain of waters. Let our soul thirst, as David thirsted, for the fountain. What is the fountain? Listen to David: "With you is the fountain of life." Let my soul say to this fountain: "When shall I come and see you face to face?" For the fountain is God himself. *Ambrose*

FURTHER READING: Psalm 56; 57; 58; 64; 65

TUESDAY

Rend your heart, and not your garments, and return to the Lord your God, for he is gracious and merciful, slow to anger and abounding in steadfast love, and repents of evil. (Joel 2:13 BCP)

CONFESSION: See page 11.

SCRIPTURE READING: John 4:43-54

⁴³After the two days he departed to Galilee. ⁴⁴For Jesus himself testified that a prophet has no honor in his own country. ⁴⁵So when he came to Galilee, the Galileans welcomed him, having seen all that he had done in Jerusalem at the feast, for they too had gone to the feast.

⁴⁶So he came again to Cana in Galilee, where he had made the water wine. And at Capernaum there was an official whose son was ill. ⁴⁷When he heard that Jesus had come from Judea to Galilee, he went and begged him to come down and heal his son, for

he was at the point of death. [48]Jesus therefore said to him, "Unless you see signs and wonders you will not believe." [49]The official said to him, "Sir, come down before my child dies." [50]Jesus said to him, "Go; your son will live." The man believed the word that Jesus spoke to him and went his way. [51]As he was going down, his servants met him and told him that his son was living. [52]So he asked them the hour when he began to mend, and they said to him, "Yesterday at the seventh hour the fever left him." [53]The father knew that was the hour when Jesus had said to him, "Your son will live"; and he himself believed, and all his household. [54]This was now the second sign that Jesus did when he had come from Judea to Galilee.

REFLECTIONS FROM THE CHURCH FATHERS

Do Not Wait for Miracles, CHRYSOSTOM. So what are we taught by these things? We are taught not to wait for miracles or to seek promises of the power of God. I see a lot of people, even now, who become more pious when, during the sufferings of a child or the sickness of a wife, they see any sign of relief. And yet, even if their child or wife did not obtain that relief, they still should persist in giving thanks and in glorifying God. Because right-minded servants and those who love their Master as they ought should run to him not only when they are pardoned but also when chastised. For this too also shows the tender care of God, since "those whom the Lord loves he also chastens." *Homilies on the Gospel of John 35.3.*

Wealth Neither Impressed Nor Deterred Jesus, GREGORY THE GREAT. In this matter we must pay careful attention to what we have learned from the testimony of another Evangelist. A centurion came to the Lord saying, "Sir, my servant is lying at home paralyzed and in great pain." Jesus immediately answered him, "I myself will come and heal him." Why is it that when the ruler asked him to come to his son, he refused to go there in person, but he promised to go in person to the servant, when the centurion had not asked him to do so? He did not condescend to be physically present to the ruler's son but did hurry to the side of the centurion's servant. Why was this, except to check our pride? We do not respect in people their nature, made in God's image, but their riches and reputation. When we consider what is important about them we scarcely regard what they are inwardly. We pay attention to what is physically displeasing about them and neglect to consider what they are. Our Redeemer, to show us that the things human beings regard highly are displeasing to the saints and that we are not to be displeased by what humans consider displeasing, refused to go to the ruler's son but was ready to go to the centurion's servant. . . . You see that one came from heaven who was not reluctant to hurry to a servant on earth, and yet we who are of the earth refuse to be humbled on earth. *Forty Gospel Homilies 28.*

CLOSING PRAYER

Into your hands, O Lord, we commit ourselves this day. Give to each one of us a watchful, a humble, and a diligent spirit that we may seek in all things to know your will, and when we know it may perform it perfectly and gladly, to the honor and glory of your Name; through Jesus Christ our Lord. Amen. *Gelasian Sacramentary*

FURTHER READING: Psalm 61; 62; 68

WEDNESDAY

†

Rend your heart, and not your garments, and return to the Lord your God, for he is gracious and merciful, slow to anger and abounding in steadfast love, and repents of evil. (Joel 2:13 BCP)

CONFESSION: See page 11.

SCRIPTURE READING: John 5:1-15

[1]After this there was a feast of the Jews, and Jesus went up to Jerusalem.

[2]Now there is in Jerusalem by the Sheep Gate a pool, in Hebrew called Bethzatha, which has five porticoes. [3]In these lay a multitude of invalids, blind, lame, paralyzed. [5]One man was there, who had been ill for thirty-eight years. [6]When Jesus saw him and knew that he had been lying there a long time, he said to him, "Do you want to be healed?" [7]The sick man answered him, "Sir, I have no man to put me into the pool when the water is troubled, and while I am going another steps down before me." [8]Jesus said to him, "Rise, take up your pallet, and walk." [9]And at once the man was healed, and he took up his pallet and walked.

Now that day was the sabbath. [10]So the Jews said to the man who was cured, "It is the sabbath, it is not lawful for you to carry your pallet." [11]But he answered them, "The man who healed me said to me, 'Take up your pallet, and walk.'" [12]They asked him, "Who is the man who said to you, 'Take up your pallet, and walk'?" [13]Now the man who had been healed did not know who it was, for Jesus had withdrawn, as there was a crowd in the place. [14]Afterward, Jesus found him in the temple, and said to him, "See, you are well!

Sin no more, that nothing worse befall you." [15]The man went away and told the Jews that it was Jesus who had healed him.

REFLECTIONS FROM THE CHURCH FATHERS

Take Up Your Bed and Govern Your Life, CAESARIUS OF ARLES. What does this mean, "take up your pallet" except carry and govern your body? Conduct that which carried you. For when you were under the dominion of sin your flesh first carried you to evil, but now since grace is in control you conduct and direct your body to what is good. In the wrong and wicked order your flesh was first in control and the soul served. But now through the mercy of Christ the soul holds sway and the flesh is subject to it in servitude. "Rise, take up your pallet, and go into your house." When you were thrown out of your house, that is, out of the land of paradise at the intervention of sin, your flesh hurled you down into the world. But now through the gift of divine mercy take up your pallet, and in every good work govern your little body and return to your house, that is, return to eternal life. . . . From it we were thrown into the exile of this world. Therefore, when you hear it said to the paralytic, "take up your pallet, and go into your house," believe that it is said to you: govern your flesh in all chastity and return to paradise, as if to your own home and your original country. *Sermon 171.1.*

Healed to a New Life in God, GREGORY OF NAZIANZUS. Yesterday you were flung upon a bed, exhausted and paralyzed, and you had no one to put you into the pool when the water should be troubled. Today you have him who is in one person man and God, or rather God and man. You were raised up from your bed, or rather you took up your bed and publicly acknowledged the benefit. Do not again be thrown on your bed by sinning. . . . But as you now are, so walk, mindful of the command. . . . Sin no more lest a worse thing happen to you if you prove yourself to be evil after the blessing you have received. *On Holy Baptism, Oration 40.33.*

CLOSING PRAYER

We beg you, Lord, to help and defend us. Deliver the oppressed, pity the insignificant, raise the fallen, show yourself to the needy, heal the sick, bring back those of your people who have gone astray, feed the hungry, lift up the weak, take off the prisoners' chains. May every nation come to know that you alone are God, that Jesus Christ is your child, that we are your people, the sheep of your pasture. *Clement of Rome*

FURTHER READING: Psalm 72; 119:73-96

THURSDAY

Rend your heart, and not your garments, and return to the Lord your God, for he is gracious and merciful, slow to anger and abounding in steadfast love, and repents of evil. (Joel 2:13 BCP)

CONFESSION: See page 11.

SCRIPTURE READING: John 5:16-29

[16]And this was why the Jews persecuted Jesus, because he did this on the sabbath. [17]But Jesus answered them, "My Father is working still, and I am working." [18]This was why the Jews sought all the more to kill him, because he not only broke the sabbath but also called God his Father, making himself equal with God.

[19]Jesus said to them, "Truly, truly, I say to you, the Son can do nothing of his own accord, but only what he sees the Father doing;

for whatever he does, that the Son does likewise. [20]For the Father loves the Son, and shows him all that he himself is doing; and greater works than these will he show him, that you may marvel. [21]For as the Father raises the dead and gives them life, so also the Son gives life to whom he will. [22]The Father judges no one, but has given all judgment to the Son, [23]that all may honor the Son, even as they honor the Father. He who does not honor the Son does not honor the Father who sent him. [24]Truly, truly, I say to you, he who hears my word and believes him who sent me, has eternal life; he does not come into judgment, but has passed from death to life.

[25]"Truly, truly, I say to you, the hour is coming, and now is, when the dead will hear the voice of the Son of God, and those who hear will live. [26]For as the Father has life in himself, so he has granted the Son also to have life in himself, [27]and has given him authority to execute judgment, because he is the Son of man. [28]Do not marvel at this; for the hour is coming when all who are in the tombs will hear his voice [29]and come forth, those who have done good, to the resurrection of life, and those who have done evil, to the resurrection of judgment."

REFLECTIONS FROM THE CHURCH FATHERS

The Judge Is Also Our Advocate, AMBROSE. But if there is fear that the judge may be too harsh, think about who your judge is. For the Father has given every judgment to Christ. Can Christ then condemn you when he redeemed you from death and offered himself on your behalf? Can he condemn you when he knows that your life is what was gained by his death? *Jacob and the Happy Life 1.6.26.*

The Care and Labor Spent on Lengthening Life, AUGUSTINE. Because people love being alive on this earth, they are promised life. And because they are very afraid of dying, they are promised a life that is eternal. . . . But we see the lovers of this present transitory life strive so hard for it, that when the fear of death looms up they do everything they can, not to eliminate death but simply to put it off. The pains a person will take, the trouble he will endure when death looms ahead, running away, going into hiding, giving everything he has and paying his ransom, struggling, enduring all sorts of torments and afflictions, bringing in doctors and whatever else a person can do! But notice how one can take endless pains and spend all of his means in order to live a little longer; but when it comes to living forever, he can do nothing. If so much care and labor then is spent on gaining a little additional length of life, how ought we to strive after life eternal? And if those people who try in every possible way to put off death are thought to be wise, even though they can only live a few days longer, how foolish are they who live in such a way that they lose the eternal day? *Sermon 127.2.*

CLOSING PRAYER

We ask you, O Lord, to be gracious to your people, that we, leaving day by day the things which displease you, may be more and more filled with the love of your commandments, and being supported by your comfort in this present life, may advance to the full enjoyment of life immortal; through Jesus Christ our Lord. Amen. *Leonine Sacramentary*

FURTHER READING: Psalm 70; 71; 74

Friday

✝

Rend your heart, and not your garments, and return to the Lord your God, for he is gracious and merciful, slow to anger and abounding in steadfast love, and repents of evil. (Joel 2:13 BCP)

Confession: See page 11.

Scripture Reading: John 5:30-40

[30]"I can do nothing on my own authority; as I hear, I judge; and my judgment is just, because I seek not my own will but the will of him who sent me. [31]If I bear witness to myself, my testimony is not true; [32]there is another who bears witness to me, and I know that the testimony which he bears to me is true. [33]You sent to John, and he has borne witness to the truth. [34]Not that the testimony which I receive is from man; but I say this that you may be saved. [35]He was a burning and shining lamp, and you were willing to rejoice for a while in his light. [36]But the testimony which I have is greater than that of John; for the works which the Father has granted me to accomplish, these very works which I am doing, bear me witness that the Father has sent me. [37]And the Father who sent me has himself borne witness to me. His voice you have never heard, his form you have never seen; [38]and you do not have his word abiding in you, for you do not believe him whom he has sent. [39]You search the scriptures, because you think that in them you have eternal life; and it is they that bear witness to me; [40]yet you refuse to come to me that you may have life."

Reflections from the Church Fathers

We Want to Do Our Own Will, Augustine. The only Son says, "I seek not my own will," and yet we want to do our own will! See how low the one who is equal to the Father humbles himself! . . . Let us then do the will of the Father, Christ and Holy Spirit, for this Trinity has one will, power and majesty. *Tractates on the Gospel of John 22.15.*

Do Not Only Read but Also Examine Scripture, CHRYSOSTOM. He tells them not to simply "read the Scriptures" but "search the Scriptures." . . . These sayings were not on the surface or out in the open but were hidden very deep like some treasure. Anyone who searches for hidden things, unless they are careful and diligent, will never find the object of their search. This is why he says, . . . "For in them you think you have eternal life," meaning that they did not reap much fruit from the Scriptures, thinking, as they did, that they should be saved by the mere reading of them, without faith. . . . And so, it was with good reason that he said "you think," because they did not actually listen to what the Scripture had to say but merely prided themselves on the bare reading. *Homilies on the Gospel of John 41.1.*

CLOSING PRAYER

Lord, inspire us to read your Scriptures and meditate upon them day and night. We beg you to give us real understanding of what we need, that we in turn may put its precepts into practice. Yet we know that understanding and good intentions are worthless, unless rooted in your graceful love. So we ask that the words of Scripture may also be not just signs on a page, but channels of grace into our hearts. *Origen*

FURTHER READING: Psalm 69; 73; 95

Saturday

✝

Rend your heart, and not your garments, and return to the Lord your God, for he is gracious and merciful, slow to anger and abounding in steadfast love, and repents of evil. (Joel 2:13 BCP)

Confession: See page 11.

Scripture Reading: John 5:40-47

[40]"Yet you refuse to come to me that you may have life. [41]I do not receive glory from men. [42]But I know that you have not the love of God within you. [43]I have come in my Father's name, and you do not receive me; if another comes in his own name, him you will receive. [44]How can you believe, who receive glory from one another and do not seek the glory that comes from the only God? [45]Do not think that I shall accuse you to the Father; it is Moses who accuses you, on whom you set your hope. [46]If you believed Moses, you would believe me, for he wrote of me. [47]But if you do not believe his writings, how will you believe my words?"

Reflections from the Church Fathers

The Glory They Give Is Useless Without the Love of God, THEODORE OF MOPSUESTIA. After he had rebuked with all these words those who did not want to believe in him, and after he had confirmed with different [arguments] those words said about him, he opportunely rejected the foolish conclusion that had followed his words by saying: I do not accept glory from human beings. But I know that you do not have the love of God in you. I have used these words not because I want glory from you or because I expect that your faith will be an advantage for me, but so that I might reprove you since you do not have the love of God. And, with the pretext of the love for God, you even eagerly persecute me as if I were vainly or even impiously boasting equality with him. So, I reprove you in order that you might turn to virtue after being rebuked. He then said aptly: *ou lambanō*, that is, "I do not accept" the glory given to me. My nature does not increase in dignity through the glory of people. *Commentary on John 2.5.41-42.*

Hunting for Honor Among People Comes Up Short, CYRIL OF ALEX- ANDRIA. He accuses the Pharisees of a love for power and of prizing honors from people. He is covertly hinting that it is exceedingly inadvisable to put the diseases of their own soul on God, who can by no means have anything to do with disease. He goes on to say that they, held fast by an empty kind of glory, thereby lose the fair- est prize, meaning faith in him. Paul speaks clearly of this too when he says, "For if I were yet pleasing people, I should not be Christ's servant." It is almost always necessarily the case that those who hunt for honors from people fail when it comes to the glory that comes from above and from the only God. *Commentary on the Gospel of John 3.2.*

CLOSING PRAYER

O God, who resists the proud and gives grace to the humble: grant us the virtue of true humility which your only-begotten Son him- self gave us the perfect example; that we may never offend you by our pride and be rejected by our self-assertion; through Jesus Christ our Lord. *Leonine Sacramentary*

FURTHER READING: Psalm 23; 27; 75; 76

Week Three

✝✝✝

Almighty God, you know that we have no power in ourselves to help ourselves: Keep us both outwardly in our bodies and inwardly in our souls, that we may be defended from all adversities which may happen to the body, and from all evil thoughts which may assault and hurt the soul; through Jesus Christ our Lord, who lives and reigns with you and the Holy Spirit, one God, for ever and ever. *Amen.* COLLECT FOR THE THIRD SUNDAY IN LENT.

SUNDAY

†

I will arise and go to my father, and I will say to him, "Father, I have sinned against heaven and before you; I am no longer worthy to be called your son." (Luke 15:18-19 BCP)

CONFESSION: See page 11.

SCRIPTURE READING: John 6:1-15

¹After this Jesus went to the other side of the Sea of Galilee, which is the Sea of Tiberias. ²And a multitude followed him, because they saw the signs which he did on those who were diseased. ³Jesus went up on the mountain, and there sat down with his disciples. ⁴Now the Passover, the feast of the Jews, was at hand. ⁵Lifting up his eyes, then, and seeing that a multitude was coming to him, Jesus said to Philip, "How are we to buy bread, so that these people may eat?" ⁶This he said to test him, for he himself knew what he would do. ⁷Philip answered him, "Two hundred denarii would not buy enough bread for each of them to get a little." ⁸One of his disciples, Andrew, Simon Peter's brother, said to him, ⁹"There is a lad here who has five barley loaves and two fish; but what are they among so many?" ¹⁰Jesus said, "Make the people sit down." Now there was much grass in the place; so the men sat down, in number about five thousand. ¹¹Jesus then took the loaves, and when he had given thanks, he distributed them to those who were seated; so also the fish, as much as they wanted. ¹²And when they had eaten their fill, he told his disciples, "Gather up the fragments left over, that nothing may be lost." ¹³So they gathered them up and filled twelve baskets with fragments from the five barley loaves, left by those who had eaten. ¹⁴When the people saw the

sign which he had done, they said, "This is indeed the prophet who is to come into the world!"

[15]Perceiving then that they were about to come and take him by force to make him king, Jesus withdrew again to the mountain by himself.

Reflections from the Church Fathers

The Creator of the Universe Will Provide, Romanus Melodus.
When Christ heard these words of His disciples,
He answered them in this way: "You are mistaken if you do not know
That I am the Creator of the universe; I provide for the world;
I now know clearly what these people need;
I see the desert and that the sun is setting;
Indeed I arranged the setting of the sun;
I understand the distress of the crowd which is here;
I know what I have in mind to do for them.
I myself shall cure their hunger, for I am

The heavenly bread of immortality. . . .
"Even though you consider carefully, can you as mere men secure nourishment,
Or can you, though you are worried, feed the people?
Or, then, if you cannot feed them, have you the power to keep silent?
I, alone, as Creator take thought for all.
I exist as good, God before the centuries.
And I provide every kind of food for all people;
But you, on beholding the multitude, are worried,
And you do not consider the One who provides abundantly,
As I am set before all, offering
The heavenly bread of immortality."
Kontakion on the Multiplication of Loaves 13.12-17.

Christ Multiplies Our Good Works, CYRIL OF ALEXANDRIA. Initially the disciples were reluctant to feed the hungry, but seeing this, the Savior gave to them in abundance from the fragments. This teaches us as well, that we, by expending a little for the glory of God, shall receive richer grace according to the saying of Christ, "a good measure, pressed down, shaken together, running over, will be put into your lap." Therefore, we must not be slothful regarding the communion of love toward our brothers and sisters but rather put away from us, as far as possible, the cowardice and fear that lead to inhospitality. Thus we might be confirmed in hope through steadfast faith in the power of God to multiply even our smallest acts of goodness. *Commentary on the Gospel of John 3.4.*

CLOSING PRAYER

O God, from whom all holy desires, all good counsels, and all just works do proceed; give unto your servants that peace which the world cannot give, that both our hearts may be set to obey your commandments, and also that, by you, we being defended from the fear of our enemies, may pass our time in rest and quietness, through the merits of Jesus Christ our Savior. Amen. *Gelasian Sacramentary*

FURTHER READING: Psalm 19; 46; 66; 67

MONDAY

✝

I will arise and go to my father, and I will say to him, "Father, I have sinned against heaven and before you; I am no longer worthy to be called your son." (Luke 15:18-19 BCP)

CONFESSION: See page 11.

SCRIPTURE READING: John 6:16-27

[16]When evening came, his disciples went down to the sea, [17]got into a boat, and started across the sea to Capernaum. It was now dark, and Jesus had not yet come to them. [18]The sea rose because a strong wind was blowing. [19]When they had rowed about three or four miles, they saw Jesus walking on the sea and drawing near to the boat. They were frightened, [20]but he said to them, "It is I; do not be afraid." [21]Then they were glad to take him into the boat, and immediately the boat was at the land to which they were going.

[22]On the next day the people who remained on the other side of the sea saw that there had been only one boat there, and that Jesus had not entered the boat with his disciples, but that his disciples had gone away alone. [23]However, boats from Tiberias came near the place where they ate the bread after the Lord had given thanks. [24]So when the people saw that Jesus was not there, nor his disciples, they themselves got into the boats and went to Capernaum, seeking Jesus.

[25]When they found him on the other side of the sea, they said to him, "Rabbi, when did you come here?" [26]Jesus answered them, "Truly, truly, I say to you, you seek me, not because you saw signs, but because you ate your fill of the loaves. [27]Do not labor for the

food which perishes, but for the food which endures to eternal life, which the Son of man will give to you; for on him has God the Father set his seal."

REFLECTIONS FROM THE CHURCH FATHERS

The Danger of Being Without Jesus in the Storm, CYRIL OF ALEXANDRIA. The circumstances of their journey drive the disciples to a more intense search for the Savior. For the deep darkness of the night troubles them, hovering like smoke on the raging waves and taking away any ability for navigation. The fierce winds, riding on the waves with a rushing sound that raises the billows high above their heads, had to trouble them more than a little bit. Yes, and through all of this, John records, "Jesus was not yet with them." This was the real danger, and Christ's absence from these voyagers was making their fear grow more and more.

Those who are not with Jesus are in a fierce tempest of a storm. They are cut off from him or at least seem to be absent from him because they have departed from his holy laws. Because of their sin they are separated from the one who is able to save. If then it is overwhelming to be in such spiritual darkness, if it is oppressive to be swamped by the bitter sea of pleasures, let us then receive Jesus. For this is what will deliver us from dangers and from death in sin. *Commentary on the Gospel of John 3.4.*

Satisfying the Flesh Instead of the Spirit, AUGUSTINE. It is as if he said, "You seek me to satisfy the flesh, not the Spirit." How many seek Jesus for no other objective than to get some kind of temporal benefit! One has a business that has run into problems, and he seeks the intercession of the clergy; another is oppressed by someone more powerful than himself, and he flies to the church. Another desires intervention with someone over whom he has little influence. One person wants this, and another person wants that. The church is filled with these kinds of people! Jesus is scarcely sought after for his own sake. . . . Here too he says, you seek me for something else; seek me for my own sake. He insinuates the truth that he himself is that food . . . "that endures to eternal life." *Tractates on the Gospel of John 25.10.*

CLOSING PRAYER

O Word of our God, I betrayed you, the Truth, with my falsehood. I betrayed you when I promised to hallow the hours that vanish away. In overtaking me, night does not find me undarkened by sin. I did indeed pray, and I thought to stand blameless at evening. But someway and somewhere my feet have stumbled and fallen; for a storm-cloud swooped on me, envious lest I be saved. Kindle for me your light, O Christ, restore me by your Presence. *Gregory of Nazianzus*

FURTHER READING: Psalm 89

~~~~~~

TUESDAY

✝

I will arise and go to my father, and I will say to him, "Father, I have sinned against heaven and before you; I am no longer worthy to be called your son." (Luke 15:18-19 BCP)

CONFESSION: See page 11.

SCRIPTURE READING: John 6:28-40

[28]Then they said to him, "What must we do, to be doing the works of God?" [29]Jesus answered them, "This is the work of God, that

you believe in him whom he has sent."

[30]So they said to him, "Then what sign do you do, that we may see, and believe you? What work do you perform? [31]Our fathers ate the manna in the wilderness; as it is written, 'He gave them bread from heaven to eat.'" [32]Jesus then said to them, "Truly, truly, I say to you, it was not Moses who gave you the bread from heaven; my Father gives you the true bread from heaven. [33]For the bread of God is that which comes down from heaven, and gives life to the world." [34]They said to him, "Lord, give us this bread always."

[35]Jesus said to them, "I am the bread of life; he who comes to me shall not hunger, and he who believes in me shall never thirst. [36]But I said to you that you have seen me and yet do not believe. [37]All that the Father gives me will come to me; and him who comes to me I will not cast out. [38]For I have come down from heaven, not to do my own will, but the will of him who sent me; [39]and this is the will of him who sent me, that I should lose nothing of all that he has given me, but raise it up at the last day. [40]For this is the will of my Father, that every one who sees the Son and believes in him should have eternal life; and I will raise him up at the last day."

REFLECTIONS FROM THE CHURCH FATHERS

Pride Casts Out, Humility Restores, AUGUSTINE. This is the reason why he does not cast out those who come to him. "For I came down from heaven not to do my own will but the will of him that sent me." The soul departed from God because it was proud. . . . Pride casts us out, humility restores us. . . . When a physician in the treatment of a disease cures certain outward symptoms but not the cause that produces them, his cure is only temporary. So long as the cause remains, the disease may return. . . . That the cause then of all diseases, that is, pride, might be eradicated, the Son of God humbled himself. Why are you proud, O man? The Son of God humbled himself for you. It might shame you, perhaps, to imitate a humble man; but imitate at least a humble God. . . . And this is the proof of his humility: "I came not to do my own will but the will of him that sent me." Pride does its own will; humility does the will of God. For this very reason, therefore, I will not cast out the one who comes to me, because I came not to do my own will, but the will of him who sent me. I came to teach humility by being humble myself. Whoever comes to me is made a member of me. Such a person is necessarily humble, because he will not do his own will but the will of God; and therefore [this person] is not cast out. He was cast out, as proud. . . . But he will not cast us out because we are members of the one who desired to be our head by teaching us humility. *Tractates on the Gospel of John 25.15-16, 18.*

The Lost Sheep Are Returned, JEROME. Christ speaks here of the whole of his humanity, which he had taken on him in its entirety at his birth. Then shall the sheep that was lost and was wandering in the lower world be carried healthy on the Savior's shoulders. And the sheep that was sick with sin shall be taken care of by the mercy of the Judge. *Against John of Jerusalem 34.*

CLOSING PRAYER

Show me, O Lord, your mercy, and delight my heart with it. Let me find you whom I so longingly seek. See, here is the man whom the robbers seized, mishandled, and left half dead on the road to Jericho. O kind-hearted Samaritan, come to my aid! I am the sheep who wandered into the wilderness—seek after me, and bring me home again to your fold. Do with me what you will, that I may stay by you all the days of my life, and praise you with all those who are with you in heaven for all eternity. *Jerome*

FURTHER READING: Psalm 94; 95; 97; 99; 100

Wednesday

†

I will arise and go to my father, and I will say to him, "Father, I have sinned against heaven and before you; I am no longer worthy to be called your son." (Luke 15:18-19 BCP)

Confession: See page 11.

Scripture Reading: John 6:41-51

[41]The Jews then murmured at him, because he said, "I am the bread which came down from heaven." [42]They said, "Is not this Jesus, the son of Joseph, whose father and mother we know? How does he now say, 'I have come down from heaven'?" [43]Jesus answered them, "Do not murmur among yourselves. [44]No one can come to me unless the Father who sent me draws him; and I will raise him up at the last day. [45]It is written in the prophets, 'And they shall all be taught by God.' Every one who has heard and learned from the Father comes to me. [46]Not that any one has seen the Father except him who is from God; he has seen the Father. [47]Truly, truly, I say to you, he who believes has eternal life. [48]I am the bread of life. [49]Your fathers ate the manna in the wilderness, and they died. [50]This is the bread which comes down from heaven, that a man may eat of it and not die. [51]I am the living bread which came down from heaven; if any one eats of this bread, he will live for ever; and the bread which I shall give for the life of the world is my flesh."

Reflections from the Church Fathers

As Beggars Before God We Ask for Bread, Augustine. You are God's beggar. I mean, we are all God's beggars when we pray. We stand in front of the great householder's gate. In fact we go so far as to prostrate ourselves, we whine and implore, wanting to receive something, and that something is God himself. What does the beggar ask from you? Bread. And you, what do you ask from God, if not Christ, who says, "I am the living bread who came down from heaven"? *Sermon 83.2.*

Many Grains Joined Together, CYPRIAN. The body of the Lord cannot be flour alone or water alone, unless both are united and joined together and compacted in the mass of one bread. In this very sacrament our people are shown to be made one, so that as many grains, collected and ground and mixed together into one mass, make one bread, so also in Christ, who is the heavenly bread, we may know that there is one body with which our number is joined and united. *Letter 62.13.*

CLOSING PRAYER

Glory to you, Lord Jesus Christ! You built your cross as a bridge over death, so that departed souls might pass from the realm of death to the realm of life. Glory to you! You put on the body of a mortal man and made it the source of life for all mortal human beings. You are alive! Your murderers handled your life like farmers: they sowed it like grain deep in the earth, waiting for it to spring up and raise with itself a multitude of men. We offer you the great, universal sacrifice of our love, and pour out before you our richest hymns and prayers. For you offered your cross to God as a sacrifice in order to make us all rich. *Ephrem the Syrian*

FURTHER READING: Psalm 101; 109:1-30; 119:121-144

THURSDAY

†

I will arise and go to my father, and I will say to him, "Father, I have sinned against heaven and before you; I am no longer worthy to be called your son." (Luke 15:18-19 BCP)

CONFESSION: See page 11.

SCRIPTURE READING: John 6:52-59

[52]The Jews then disputed among themselves, saying, "How can this man give us his flesh to eat?" [53]So Jesus said to them, "Truly, truly, I say to you, unless you eat the flesh of the Son of man and drink his blood, you have no life in you; [54]he who eats my flesh and drinks my blood has eternal life, and I will raise him up at the last day. [55]For my flesh is food indeed, and my blood is drink indeed. [56]He who eats my flesh and drinks my blood abides in me, and I in him. [57]As the living Father sent me, and I live because of the Father, so he who eats me will live because of me. [58]This is the bread which came down from heaven, not such as the fathers ate and died; he who eats this bread will live for ever." [59]This he said in the synagogue, as he taught at Capernaum.

REFLECTIONS FROM THE CHURCH FATHERS

Real Satisfaction, AUGUSTINE. Or think of it this way: Whereas people desire meat and drink to satisfy hunger and thirst, real satisfaction is produced only by that meat and drink that make the receivers of it immortal and incorruptible. He's talking here about the fellowship of the saints where there is peace and unity, full and perfect. Therefore . . . our Lord has chosen for the types of his body and blood things that become one out of many. Bread is a quantity of grains united into one mass, wine a quantity of grapes squeezed together. Then he explains what it is to eat his body and drink his blood: "He that eats my flesh and drinks my blood dwells in me and I in him." So then to partake of that meat and that drink is to dwell in Christ and Christ in you. Whoever does not dwell in Christ, and in whom Christ does not dwell, neither eats his flesh nor drinks his blood; rather, he eats and drinks the sacrament of it to his own damnation. *Tractates on the Gospel of John 26.17-18.*

Eat and Drink of the One Who Is Life, CYRIL OF ALEXANDRIA. O sublime condescension! The Creator gives himself to his creatures for their delight. Life bestows itself on mortals as food and drink. "Come, eat my body," he exhorts us, "and drink the wine I have mingled for you. I have prepared myself as food. I have mingled myself for those who desire me. Of my own will I became flesh and have become a partaker of your flesh and blood. . . . Eat of me as I am life, and live, for this is what I desire. . . . Eat my bread, for I am the life-giving grain of the wheat, and I am the bread of life. Drink the wine I have mingled for you, for I am the draught of immortality. . . . I am the true vine; drink my joy, the wine that I have mingled for you." *Meditation on the Mystical Supper 10.*

CLOSING PRAYER

O God, the Life of the faithful, the strong Helper of them that call upon you: listen to our supplications; and as you put within us a hearty desire to pray, so grant us, O most Loving, your aid and comfort in our prayers; and may the souls that thirst for your promises, be filled from your abundance; through Jesus Christ our Lord. Amen. *Gelasian Sacramentary*

FURTHER READING: Psalm 69; 73

FRIDAY

†

I will arise and go to my father, and I will say to him, "Father, I have sinned against heaven and before you; I am no longer worthy to be called your son." (Luke 15:18-19 BCP)

CONFESSION: See page 11.

SCRIPTURE READING: John 6:60-71

[60]Many of his disciples, when they heard it, said, "This is a hard saying; who can listen to it?" [61]But Jesus, knowing in himself that his disciples murmured at it, said to them, "Do you take offense at this? [62]Then what if you were to see the Son of man ascending where he was before? [63]It is the spirit that gives life, the flesh is of no avail; the words that I have spoken to you are spirit and life. [64]But there are some of you that do not believe." For Jesus knew from the first who those were that did not believe, and who it was that would betray him. [65]And he said, "This is why I told you that no one can come to me unless it is granted him by the Father."

[66]After this many of his disciples drew back and no longer went about with him. [67]Jesus said to the twelve, "Do you also wish to go away?" [68]Simon Peter answered him, "Lord, to whom shall we go? You have the words of eternal life; [69]and we have believed, and have come to know, that you are the Holy One of God." [70]Jesus answered them, "Did I not choose you, the twelve, and one of you is a devil?" [71]He spoke of Judas the son of Simon Iscariot, for he, one of the twelve, was to betray him.

REFLECTIONS FROM THE CHURCH FATHERS

Only the Spirit Can Give Life, TERTULLIAN. If he says that "the flesh profits nothing," then the meaning must take direction from the context of that remark. For seeing that they regarded his speech as hard and unbearable, as though he had really prescribed his flesh for them to eat, since his purpose was to assign the establishment of salvation to the Spirit, he first said, "It is the spirit that gives life," and only then added, "the flesh profits nothing"—toward the giving of life, of course. He also proceeds to state how he wishes "the Spirit" to be understood. "The words that I have spoken to you are spirit and life." . . . And so, when establishing his teaching as the Lifegiver (because the Word is spirit and life), he also said that it is his flesh, because the Word also was made flesh. We ought therefore to desire him in order that we may have life. We ought to devour him with the ear, and to ruminate on him with the mind and to digest him by faith. *On the Resurrection of the Flesh 37.*

Good Produced from Evil, Augustine. Evil people make evil use of all the good creations of God. Good people, on the other hand, make good use of the evil actions of the wicked. And who is as good as the one and only God? . . . For as the wicked turn the good works of God to an evil use, so inversely God turns the evil works of human beings to good. What can be worse than what Judas did? He was chosen as the treasurer among the Twelve who would dispense gifts to the poor. But instead of being thankful for so great an honor and favor, he took the money and lost righteousness. Being dead, he betrayed life. The one he followed as a disciple he betrayed as an enemy. Yet our Lord made a good use of his wickedness, allowing himself to be betrayed so that he might redeem us. . . . If God employs the evil works of the devil himself for good, whatever the evil person does by making bad use of God's good gifts only hurts himself. It in no way contradicts the goodness of God. *Tractates on the Gospel of John 27.10.*

CLOSING PRAYER

Almighty God, who resists the proud and gives grace to the humble: send your Holy Spirit and let that mind be in us, which was also in Christ Jesus, that we may be meek and lowly of heart, and never by our foolish pride provoke your indignation; but, receiving into humble and thankful hearts the gifts of your providence and of your grace, may thereby be continually refreshed. Teach us not to think of ourselves more highly than we ought to think; to be modest in speech, just and merciful in action, and benevolent unto all. Let us prefer nothing to him, who preferred nothing to our salvation; but grant us that adhering inseparably to his Kingdom, and standing bravely by his Cross, we may be found faithful unto death, and at the end may be admitted into the joy of his most blessed presence. Amen. *Cyprian*

FURTHER READING: Psalm 95; 102; 107:1-32

◇◇ ﹥ ﹥﹥◇◇◇◇◇◇ ﹥﹥◇◇◇◇◇◇ ﹥﹥◇◇◇◇◇◇ ﹥﹥◇◇◇◇◇◇ ﹥﹥◇◇◇◇◇◇ ﹥﹥◇◇◇◇◇◇ ﹥﹥◇◇

SATURDAY

†

I will arise and go to my father, and I will say to him, "Father, I have sinned against heaven and before you; I am no longer worthy to be called your son." (Luke 15:18-19 BCP)

CONFESSION: See page 11.

SCRIPTURE READING: John 7:1-13

[1]After this Jesus went about in Galilee; he would not go about in

Judea, because the Jews sought to kill him. ²Now the Jews' feast of Tabernacles was at hand. ³So his brothers said to him, "Leave here and go to Judea, that your disciples may see the works you are doing. ⁴For no man works in secret if he seeks to be known openly. If you do these things, show yourself to the world." ⁵For even his brothers did not believe in him. ⁶Jesus said to them, "My time has not yet come, but your time is always here. ⁷The world cannot hate you, but it hates me because I testify of it that its works are evil. ⁸Go to the feast yourselves; I am not going up to this feast, for my time has not yet fully come." ⁹So saying, he remained in Galilee.

¹⁰But after his brothers had gone up to the feast, then he also went up, not publicly but in private. ¹¹The Jews were looking for him at the feast, and saying, "Where is he?" ¹²And there was much muttering about him among the people. While some said, "He is a good man," others said, "No, he is leading the people astray." ¹³Yet for fear of the Jews no one spoke openly of him.

Reflections from the Church Fathers

The Time for Glory Is Not Yet Come, Augustine. They advised him to pursue glory and not allow himself to remain in concealment and obscurity, appealing to altogether worldly and secular motives. . . . But our Lord was laying down another road to that very exaltation, that is, humility. . . . "My time," he says, that is, the time of my glory when I shall come to judge on high is not yet come; but your time, that is, the glory of the world, is always ready. . . . And let us, who are the Lord's body, when insulted by the lovers of this world, say, your time is ready: ours is not yet come. *Tractates on the Gospel of John 28.5-7.*

Reproof Naturally Brings Hatred, Cyril of Alexandria. For the world loves sin. The Lord is a corrector of those who do not act rightly. And correction must often be attained by reproof. For the mere calling of a sin a sin is already a rebuke to those who love that sin, and the reproof of iniquity already lays blame on those who have that iniquity. And so, when necessity calls for the teacher to administer reproof, and the mode of cure requires it to happen in this way, and the one being instructed by such a rebuke against his will is exceedingly angry, then the ills of hatred must surely arise. Therefore, the Savior says that he is hated by the world in that it cannot yet bear exhortation with rebuke when it really needs to do so in order to profit from it. For the mind that is in bondage to evil pleasures gets quite angry with the advice that would persuade it to shape up. And the Savior says these things, not altogether saying that he will not go to Jerusalem or refusing to give the reproofs that may be profitable to the sinners, but minded to do this too and everything else at the proper time. *Commentary on the Gospel of John 4.5.*

CLOSING PRAYER

May God, the Lord, bless us with all heavenly benediction, and make us pure and holy in His sight. May the riches of His glory abound in us. May He instruct us with the word of truth, inform us with the Gospel of salvation, and enrich us with His love, through Jesus Christ, our Lord, Amen. *Gelasian Sacramentary*

FURTHER READING: Psalm 33; 107:33-43; 108

Week Four

Gracious Father, whose blessed Son Jesus Christ came down from heaven to be the true bread which gives life to the world: Evermore give us this bread, that he may live in us, and we in him; who lives and reigns with you and the Holy Spirit, one God, now and for ever. *Amen.*
COLLECT FOR THE FOURTH SUNDAY IN LENT.

SUNDAY

✝

To the Lord our God belong mercy and forgiveness, because we have rebelled against him and have not obeyed the voice of the Lord our God by following his laws which he set before us. (Daniel 9:9-10 BCP)

CONFESSION: See page II.

SCRIPTURE READING: John 7:14-36

¹⁴About the middle of the feast Jesus went up into the temple and taught. ¹⁵The Jews marveled at it, saying, "How is it that this man has learning, when he has never studied?" ¹⁶So Jesus answered them, "My teaching is not mine, but his who sent me; ¹⁷if any man's will is to do his will, he shall know whether the teaching is from God or whether I am speaking on my own authority. ¹⁸He who speaks on his own authority seeks his own glory; but he who seeks the glory of him who sent him is true, and in him there is no falsehood. ¹⁹Did not Moses give you the law? Yet none of you keeps the law. Why do you seek to kill me?" ²⁰The people answered, "You have a demon! Who is seeking to kill you?" ²¹Jesus answered them, "I did one deed, and you all marvel at it. ²²Moses gave you circumcision (not that it is from Moses, but from the fathers), and you circumcise a man upon the sabbath. ²³If on the sabbath a man receives circumcision, so that the law of Moses may not be broken, are you angry with me because on the sabbath I made a man's whole body well? ²⁴Do not judge by appearances, but judge with right judgment."

²⁵Some of the people of Jerusalem therefore said, "Is not this the man whom they seek to kill? ²⁶And here he is, speaking openly,

and they say nothing to him! Can it be that the authorities really know that this is the Christ? [27]Yet we know where this man comes from; and when the Christ appears, no one will know where he comes from." [28]So Jesus proclaimed, as he taught in the temple, "You know me, and you know where I come from? But I have not come of my own accord; he who sent me is true, and him you do not know. [29]I know him, for I come from him, and he sent me." [30]So they sought to arrest him; but no one laid hands on him, because his hour had not yet come. [31]Yet many of the people believed in him; they said, "When the Christ appears, will he do more signs than this man has done?"

[32]The Pharisees heard the crowd thus muttering about him, and the chief priests and Pharisees sent officers to arrest him. [33]Jesus then said, "I shall be with you a little longer, and then I go to him who sent me; [34]you will seek me and you will not find me; where I am you cannot come." [35]The Jews said to one another, "Where does this man intend to go that we shall not find him? Does he intend to go to the Dispersion among the Greeks and teach the Greeks? [36]What does he mean by saying, 'You will seek me and you will not find me,' and, 'Where I am you cannot come'?"

REFLECTIONS FROM THE CHURCH FATHERS

Honor and Truth Needed in Judging, AUGUSTINE. It requires a lot of work in this world to stay clear of the vice our Lord has noted in this place. It is difficult to maintain sound judgment and to stop judging by appearances. His admonition to the Jews is an admonition to us as well. . . . Let us not judge, then, by appearances, but hold to sound judgment. But who is it who does not judge according to appearances? It is the one who loves [all] equally. When there is equal love for all, then we do not accept people on the basis of who they are. We are not talking about a situation where we honor people in a different way because of their different degrees of status. This is not an instance where we should be afraid that we are accepting people on the basis [of who they are]. For instance, there may be a case to decide between father and son. We should not put the son on an equal footing with the father in point of *honor*. But, in respect of *truth*, if the son has the better cause, we should give him the preference. In this way we give each their due so that justice does not destroy merit. *Tractates on the Gospel of John 30.7-8.*

A Stern Warning, CYRIL OF ALEXANDRIA. Here Jesus is saying: I was sent to give you life, and with long suffering to bring back to God those who had stumbled through sin. I came to remove death which had fallen upon human nature because of transgression. I came to instill the divine and heavenly light in those in darkness and, moreover, to preach the gospel to the poor, to give recovery of sight to the blind, to preach deliverance to the captives, to proclaim the acceptable year of the Lord. But, since it seems good to you in your senselessness to drive away the one who offers you such a rich bounty of heavenly goods, after a little while I will take myself back to him from whom I came, and you shall repent. Then, consumed by unavailing hindsight you will weep bitterly for yourselves and while you eagerly look to find the giver of life, you shall not be able to enjoy the one for whom you long. Having once turned aside and departed from my love toward you, I shall wholly deny you that which you seek. *Commentary on the Gospel of John 5.1.*

CLOSING PRAYER

May God the Father, and the eternal High Priest Jesus Christ, build us up in faith and truth and love, and grant us our portion among the saints with all those who believe on our Lord Jesus Christ. We pray for all saints, for kings and rulers, for the enemies of the cross of Christ, and for ourselves we pray that our fruit may abound and we may be made perfect in Christ Jesus our Lord. Amen. *Polycarp*

FURTHER READING: Psalm 34; 93; 96

<><><><><><><><><><><><><><><><><><><><><><><><><><>

MONDAY

†

To the Lord our God belong mercy and forgiveness, because we have rebelled against him and have not obeyed the voice of the Lord our God by following his laws which he set before us. (Daniel 9:9-10 BCP)

CONFESSION: See page 11.

SCRIPTURE READING: John 7:37-52

[37]On the last day of the feast, the great day, Jesus stood up and proclaimed, "If any one thirst, let him come to me and drink. [38]He who believes in me, as the scripture has said, 'Out of his heart shall flow rivers of living water.'" [39]Now this he said about the Spirit, which those who believed in him were to receive; for as yet the Spirit had not been given, because Jesus was not yet glorified.

[40]When they heard these words, some of the people said, "This is really the prophet." [41]Others said, "This is the Christ." But some said, "Is the Christ to come from Galilee? [42]Has not the scripture said that the Christ is descended from David, and comes from Bethlehem, the village where David was?" [43]So there was a division among the people over him. [44]Some of them wanted to ar-

rest him, but no one laid hands on him.

⁴⁵The officers then went back to the chief priests and Pharisees, who said to them, "Why did you not bring him?" ⁴⁶The officers answered, "No man ever spoke like this man!" ⁴⁷The Pharisees answered them, "Are you led astray, you also? ⁴⁸Have any of the authorities or of the Pharisees believed in him? ⁴⁹But this crowd, who do not know the law, are accursed." ⁵⁰Nicode'mus, who had gone to him before, and who was one of them, said to them, ⁵¹"Does our law judge a man without first giving him a hearing and learning what he does?" ⁵²They replied, "Are you from Galilee too? Search and you will see that no prophet is to rise from Galilee."

REFLECTIONS FROM THE CHURCH FATHERS

Wisdom as the Fountain of Spiritual Grace, AMBROSE. As Wisdom is the fountain of life, it is also the fountain of spiritual grace. It is also the fountain of other virtues that guide us to the course of eternal life. Therefore, the stream that irrigates paradise rises from the soul when well-tilled, but not from the soul that lies uncultivated. The results therefore are fruit trees of diverse virtues. There are four principal trees that constitute the divisions of Wisdom. These are the well-known four principal virtues: prudence, temperance, fortitude and justice. . . . Wisdom acts as the source from which these four rivers take their rise, producing streams that are composed of these virtues. *On Paradise 3.14.*

Only the Living God Could Have Spoken Like This, ATHANASIUS. They perceived that this was not a mere man like themselves, but that this was he who gave water to the saints and that it was he who was announced by the prophet Isaiah. For he was truly the splendor of the light, and the Word of God, the river that flowed from the fountains and watered the paradise of old. But now, to all he gives the same gift of the Spirit and says, "If anyone thirst, let him come to me and drink. Whoever believes on me, as the Scripture says, rivers of living water shall flow out of his belly." This was not for [a] man to say but for the living God, who truly promises life and gives the Holy Spirit. *Festal Letter 44.*

CLOSING PRAYER

I ask you, good Jesus, that as you have graciously granted to me here on earth sweetly to partake of the words of your wisdom and knowledge, so you will promise me that I may some time come to you, the fountain of all wisdom, and always appear before your face, who lives and reigns, world without end. *The Venerable Bede*

FURTHER READING: Psalm 77; 79; 80

TUESDAY

†

To the Lord our God belong mercy and forgiveness, because we have rebelled against him and have not obeyed the voice of the Lord our God by following his laws which he set before us. (Daniel 9:9-10 BCP)

CONFESSION: See page 11.

SCRIPTURE READING: John 7:53–8:11

[53]They went each to his own house,

John 8

[1]but Jesus went to the Mount of Olives. [2]Early in the morning he came again to the temple; all the people came to him, and he sat

down and taught them. ³The scribes and the Pharisees brought a woman who had been caught in adultery, and placing her in the midst ⁴they said to him, "Teacher, this woman has been caught in the act of adultery. ⁵Now in the law Moses commanded us to stone such. What do you say about her?" ⁶This they said to test him, that they might have some charge to bring against him. Jesus bent down and wrote with his finger on the ground. ⁷And as they continued to ask him, he stood up and said to them, "Let him who is without sin among you be the first to throw a stone at her." ⁸And once more he bent down and wrote with his finger on the ground. ⁹But when they heard it, they went away, one by one, beginning with the eldest, and Jesus was left alone with the woman standing before him. ¹⁰Jesus looked up and said to her, "Woman, where are they? Has no one condemned you?" ¹¹She said, "No one, Lord." And Jesus said, "Neither do I condemn you; go, and do not sin again."

Reflections from the Church Fathers

A Humble Examination, Bede. In line with our usual human way of doing things, we can understand that the reason why the Lord might wish to bend before his unprincipled tempters and to write on the ground was that by directing his look elsewhere he might give them the freedom to go away. He foresaw that as they had been astounded by his answer, they would be more inclined to depart quickly than to ask him more questions. . . .

Figuratively speaking, the fact that both before and after he gave his opinion he bent and wrote on the ground admonishes us that both before we rebuke a sinning neighbor and after we have rendered to him the ministry of due correction, we should subject ourselves to a suitably humble examination, lest perhaps we be entangled in the same things that we censure in [our neighbors] or in any other sort of misdeeds. For it often comes about, for example, that people who publicly judge a murderer to be a sinner may not perceive the worse evil of the hatred with which they themselves despoil someone in secret. People who bring an accusation against a fornicator may ignore the plague of the pride with which they congratulate themselves for their own chastity. People who condemn a drunkard may not see the venom of envy with which they themselves are eaten away. In dangers of this sort, what saving remedy is left for us except that, when we look at some other sinner, we immediately bend down—that is, we humbly observe how we would be cast down by our frail condition if divine benevolence did not keep us from falling? Let us write with a finger on the ground—that is, let us meticulously ponder with discrimination whether we can say with blessed Job, "For our heart does not censure us in all our life," and let us painstakingly remember that if our heart censures us, God is greater than our heart and he knows all things. *Homilies on the Gospels 1.25.*

God Is Both Merciful and Just, AUGUSTINE. "Neither will I condemn you." What is this, O Lord? Do you therefore favor sins? Not so, evidently. Mark what follows: "Go and sin no more." Therefore the Lord did also condemn, but condemned sins, not the sinner. For if he was a patron of sin, he would say, Neither will I condemn you; go, live as you will; be secure in my deliverance, however much you will to sin. I will deliver you from all punishment even of hell, and from the tormentors of the infernal world. He did not say this. Let them pay attention, then, who love his gentleness in the Lord, and let them fear his truth. . . . The Lord is gentle, the Lord is long suffering, the Lord is full of pity; but the Lord is also just, the Lord is also true. He bestows on you an interval for correction, but you love the delay of judgment more than the amendment of your ways. Were you a bad person yesterday? Today be a good person. Have you gone on in your wickedness today? At any rate, change tomorrow. You always expect and make exceedingly great promises to yourself, [presuming on] the mercy of God. It is as if he, who has promised you pardon through repentance, promised you also a longer life. How do you know what tomorrow may bring? Rightly you say in your heart: When I shall have corrected my ways, God will put all my sins away. . . . God has promised pardon to anyone who amends his life. But show me where God has promised you a long life. *Tractates on the Gospel of John 33.6-7.*

Closing Prayer

O Lord, you have mercy on all; take away from me my sins, and mercifully set me ablaze with the fire of your Holy Spirit. Take away from me the heart of stone, and give me a human heart, a heart to love and adore you, a heart to delight in you, to follow and enjoy you, for Christ's sake. Amen. *Jerome*

Further Reading: Psalm 78

Wednesday

To the Lord our God belong mercy and forgiveness, because we have rebelled against him and have not obeyed the voice of the Lord our God by following his laws which he set before us. (Daniel 9:9-10 BCP)

Confession: See page 11.

Scripture Reading: John 8:12-20

¹²Again Jesus spoke to them, saying, "I am the light of the world;

he who follows me will not walk in darkness, but will have the light of life." [13]The Pharisees then said to him, "You are bearing witness to yourself; your testimony is not true." [14]Jesus answered, "Even if I do bear witness to myself, my testimony is true, for I know whence I have come and whither I am going, but you do not know whence I come or whither I am going. [15]You judge according to the flesh, I judge no one. [16]Yet even if I do judge, my judgment is true, for it is not I alone that judge, but I and he who sent me. [17]In your law it is written that the testimony of two men is true; [18]I bear witness to myself, and the Father who sent me bears witness to me." [19]They said to him therefore, "Where is your Father?" Jesus answered, "You know neither me nor my Father; if you knew me, you would know my Father also." [20]These words he spoke in the treasury, as he taught in the temple; but no one arrested him, because his hour had not yet come.

REFLECTIONS FROM THE CHURCH FATHERS

The Children of Perfect Light, GREGORY OF NAZIANZUS. Listen to the voice of God, which sounds so exceedingly clear to me—I who am both disciple and master of these mysteries. This is how I hope to God it may sound to you: "I am the Light of the world." Therefore approach him and be enlightened, and do not let your faces be ashamed, being signed with the true Light. It is a season of new birth; let us be born again. It is a time of reformation; let us receive again the first Adam. Let us not remain what we are, but let us become what we once were. The Light shines in darkness in this life and in the flesh. It is chased by the darkness but is not overtaken by it. I am referring to the power of the enemy that leaps up in its shamelessness against the visible Adam. But it encounters God and is defeated. Let us put away the darkness so that we may draw near to the Light and may then become perfect Light, the children of perfect Light. *On the Holy Lights, Oration 39.2.*

Splendor of the Eternal Light, ANONYMOUS.
O Dayspring,
Splendor of the Eternal Light, and Sun of Justice.
Come and enlighten those who sit in darkness and in the shadow
of death.
O Oriens Antiphon of Advent.

CLOSING PRAYER

O Lord, the helper of the helpless, the hope of those who are past
hope, the Savior of the tempest-tossed, the harbor of the voyagers,
the physician of the sick; you know each soul and our prayer, each
home and its need; become to each one of us what we most dearly
require, receiving us all into your kingdom, making us children of
light; and pour on us your peace and love, O Lord our God. Amen.
From the Liturgy of St. Basil the Great

FURTHER READING: Psalm 81; 82; 119:97-120

THURSDAY

To the Lord our God belong mercy and forgiveness, because
we have rebelled against him and have not obeyed the voice of
the Lord our God by following his laws which he set before us.
(Daniel 9:9-10 BCP)

CONFESSION: See page 11.

Scripture Reading: John 8:21-32

[21]Again he said to them, "I go away, and you will seek me and die in your sin; where I am going, you cannot come." [22]Then said the Jews, "Will he kill himself, since he says, 'Where I am going, you cannot come'?" [23]He said to them, "You are from below, I am from above; you are of this world, I am not of this world. [24]I told you that you would die in your sins, for you will die in your sins unless you believe that I am he." [25]They said to him, "Who are you?" Jesus said to them, "Even what I have told you from the beginning. [26]I have much to say about you and much to judge; but he who sent me is true, and I declare to the world what I have heard from him." [27]They did not understand that he spoke to them of the Father. [28]So Jesus said, "When you have lifted up the Son of man, then you will know that I am he, and that I do nothing on my own authority but speak thus as the Father taught me. [29]And he who sent me is with me; he has not left me alone, for I always do what is pleasing to him." [30]As he spoke thus, many believed in him.

[31]Jesus then said to the Jews who had believed in him, "If you continue in my word, you are truly my disciples, [32]and you will know the truth, and the truth will make you free."

Reflections from the Church Fathers

Testing the Faith of the Believers, CHRYSOSTOM. Beloved, our condition needs much endurance; and endurance is best produced when doctrines are deeply rooted. For just as there is no wind that is able to tear up an oak tree by its assaults because it sends down its root deep into the earth, so too the soul that is nailed by the fear of God—not just rooted but nailed—will not be able to be overturned. . . . Our Lord wanted to test the faith of those who believed so that it might not be merely superficial, and so he digs deeper into their souls by a more striking word. . . . And so, when he said, "If you continue," he made it clear what was in their hearts. He knew that some believed but would not continue. And he makes them a magnificent promise, that is, that they shall become his disciples indeed. These words are a tacit rebuke to some who had believed and afterwards withdrawn because they could not continue. *Homilies on the Gospel of John 54.1.*

The Importance of Patience and Perseverance, CYPRIAN. We must endure and persevere, beloved brothers, so that once we have the hope of truth and freedom, we may actually attain them. For the very fact that we are Christians is the substance of faith and hope. But if hope and faith are going to achieve their result, there must be patience. For we are not following after present but future glory. . . . Therefore, waiting and patience are needed so that we may fulfill what we have begun to be and may receive what we believe and hope for according to God's own appearing. *The Good of Patience 9.13.*

CLOSING PRAYER

Grant your servants, O God, to be set on fire with your Spirit, strengthened by your power, illuminated by your splendor, filled with your grace, and to go forward by your help. Give them, O Lord, a right faith, perfect love, true humility. Grant, O Lord, that there may be in us simple affection, brave patience, persevering obedience, perpetual peace, a pure mind, a right and honest heart, a good will, a holy conscience, spiritual strength, a life unspotted and unblameable; and after having strongfully finished our course, may we be enabled happily to enter your kingdom; through Jesus Christ our Lord. Amen. *Gallican Sacramentary*

FURTHER READING: Psalm 42; 43; 83; 85; 86

Friday

✝

To the Lord our God belong mercy and forgiveness, because we have rebelled against him and have not obeyed the voice of the Lord our God by following his laws which he set before us. (Daniel 9:9-10 BCP)

CONFESSION: See page 11.

SCRIPTURE READING: John 8:47-59

[47]"He who is of God hears the words of God; the reason why you do not hear them is that you are not of God."

[48]The Jews answered him, "Are we not right in saying that you are a Samaritan and have a demon?" [49]Jesus answered, "I have not a demon; but I honor my Father, and you dishonor me. [50]Yet I do not seek my own glory; there is One who seeks it and he will be the judge. [51]Truly, truly, I say to you, if any one keeps my word, he will never see death." [52]The Jews said to him, "Now we know that you have a demon. Abraham died, as did the prophets; and you say, 'If any one keeps my word, he will never taste death.' [53]Are you greater than our father Abraham, who died? And the prophets died! Who do you claim to be?" [54]Jesus answered, "If I glorify myself, my glory is nothing; it is my Father who glorifies me, of whom you say that he is your God. [55]But you have not known him; I know him. If I said, I do not know him, I should be a liar like you; but I do know him and I keep his word. [56]Your father Abraham rejoiced that he was to see my day; he saw it and was glad." [57]The Jews then said to him, "You are not yet fifty years old, and have you seen Abraham?" [58]Jesus said to them, "Truly, truly, I say to you, before Abraham was, I am." [59]So they

took up stones to throw at him; but Jesus hid himself, and went out of the temple.

REFLECTIONS FROM THE CHURCH FATHERS

Hear with the Ears of Your Heart, GREGORY THE GREAT. Let each one of you then consider within himself if this voice of God prevails in the ears of his heart. Then he will recognize whether he is now of God. There are some who do not choose to hear God's commands even with their bodily ears. There are others who do this but do not embrace them with their heart's desire. There are still others who receive God's words readily, yes, and are touched, even to tears. But afterwards they go back to their sins again and therefore cannot be said to hear the word of God, because they neglect to practice it. *Forty Gospel Homilies 16.*

Bear Insults When Directed at Yourself, but Not at God, CHRYSOSTOM. Where there was need to instruct them, to pull down their excessive insolence, to teach them not to be proud because of Abraham—at these times he was vehement. But when it was necessary that he should bear insults he was extremely gentle. . . . And so he teaches us to avenge insults offered to God but to overlook those that are directed at ourselves. *Homilies on the Gospel of John 55.1.*

CLOSING PRAYER

You only I love; you only I follow; you only I seek; you only am I ready to serve. Because you alone are justly Lord, I desire to be under your rule. Command, I ask you, as you will, but heal and open my ears that I may hear your voice. Heal and open my eyes that I may see your beckoning. Tell me where I must go that I may see you; and I hope to do all that you command. Receive, I pray you, your fugitive, most clement Father and Lord. Enough have I served your enemies whom you have put under your feet. Enough have I been the plaything of deceits. Receive me, your servant, now fleeing from these things. *Augustine*

FURTHER READING: Psalm 88; 91; 92; 95

SATURDAY

✝

To the Lord our God belong mercy and forgiveness, because we have rebelled against him and have not obeyed the voice of the Lord our God by following his laws which he set before us. (Daniel 9:9-10 BCP)

CONFESSION: See page 11.

SCRIPTURE READING: John 9:1-17

[1]As he passed by, he saw a man blind from his birth. [2]And his disciples asked him, "Rabbi, who sinned, this man or his parents, that he was born blind?" [3]Jesus answered, "It was not that this man sinned, or his parents, but that the works of God might be made manifest in him. [4]We must work the works of him who sent me, while it is day; night comes, when no one can work. [5]As long as I am in the world, I am the light of the world." [6]As he said this, he spat on the ground and made clay of the spittle and anointed the man's eyes with the clay, [7]saying to him, "Go, wash in the pool of Siloam" (which means Sent). So he went and washed and came back seeing. [8]The neighbors and those who had seen him before as a beggar, said, "Is not this the man who used to sit and beg?" [9]Some said, "It is he"; others said, "No, but he is like him." He said,

"I am the man." [10]They said to him, "Then how were your eyes opened?" [11]He answered, "The man called Jesus made clay and anointed my eyes and said to me, 'Go to Siloam and wash'; so I went and washed and received my sight." [12]They said to him, "Where is he?" He said, "I do not know."

[13]They brought to the Pharisees the man who had formerly been blind. [14]Now it was a sabbath day when Jesus made the clay and opened his eyes. [15]The Pharisees again asked him how he had received his sight. And he said to them, "He put clay on my eyes, and I washed, and I see." [16]Some of the Pharisees said, "This man is not from God, for he does not keep the sabbath." But others said, "How can a man who is a sinner do such signs?" There was a division among them. [17]So they again said to the blind man, "What do you say about him, since he has opened your eyes?" He said, "He is a prophet."

REFLECTIONS FROM THE CHURCH FATHERS

You Too Come to Siloam, AMBROSE. Again, I ask you: What is he trying to convey to us by spitting on the ground, mixing his saliva with clay and putting it on the eyes of a blind man, saying, "Go and wash yourself in the pool of Siloam (a name that means 'sent')"? What is the meaning of the Lord's action in this? Surely one of great significance, since the person whom Jesus touches receives more than just his sight.

In one instant we see both the power of his divinity and the strength of his holiness. As the divine light, he touched this man and enlightened him. As priest, by an action symbolizing baptism he wrought in him his work of redemption. The only reason for his mixing clay with the saliva and smearing it on the eyes of the blind man was to remind you that he who restored the man to health by anointing his eyes with clay is the very one who fashioned the first man out of clay, and that this clay that is our flesh can receive the light of eternal life through the sacrament of baptism.

You, too, should come to Siloam, that is, to him who was sent by the Father, as he says in the Gospel: "My teaching is not my own; it comes from him who sent me." Let Christ wash you, and you will then see. Come and be baptized, it is time; come quickly, and you too will be able to say, "I went and washed"; you will be able to say, "I was blind, and now I can see." And, as the blind man said when his eyes began to receive the light, you too can say, "The night is almost over and the day is at hand." *Letter 67.4-6.*

The Gift of Sight and the Gift of Faith, CYRIL OF ALEXANDRIA. Here, it is as though the man is saying: I will prove to you that the power of the Healer was not exerted in vain. I will not deny the favor I received, for I now possess what I formerly longed for. I who was blind from birth and afflicted from the womb, having been anointed with clay, am healed, and I see. That is, I do not merely show you my eye opened, concealing the darkness in its depth, but I really see. From now on I am able to look at things that formerly I could only hear about. Look! The bright light of the sun is shining around me. Look! The beauty of strange sights surrounds my eye. A short time ago I scarcely knew what Jerusalem was like. Now I see the temple of God glittering within it, and I behold in its midst the truly venerable altar. And if I stood outside the gate, I could look around on the country of Judea and recognize one thing as a hill and another as a tree. And when the time changes to evening, my eye will no longer fail to notice the beauty of the nighttime sky, the brilliant company of the stars and the golden light of the moon. When I do, I shall be amazed at the skill of him who made them "from the greatness and beauty of created things." I as well as others shall acknowledge the great Creator. *Commentary on the Gospel of John 6.1.*

CLOSING PRAYER

Unto you will I offer up an offering of praise. Late have I loved you, O Beauty ever old and ever new. You were within me and I without, and there I sought you. You were with me when I was not with you. You called and cried to me, and pierced my deafness. You shone and glowed, and dispelled my blindness. You touched me, and I burned for your peace. *Augustine*

FURTHER READING: Psalm 87; 90; 136

Week Five

✝✝✝

Almighty God, you alone can bring into order the unruly wills and affections of sinners: Grant your people grace to love what you command and desire what you promise; that, among the swift and varied changes of the world, our hearts may surely there be fixed where true joys are to be found; through Jesus Christ our Lord, who lives and reigns with you and the Holy Spirit, one God, now and for ever. *Amen.* COLLECT FOR THE FIFTH SUNDAY IN LENT.

SUNDAY

†

Jesus said, "If anyone would come after me, let him deny himself and take up his cross and follow me." (Mark 8:34 BCP)

CONFESSION: See page 11.

SCRIPTURE READING: John 9:18-34

18The Jews did not believe that he had been blind and had received his sight, until they called the parents of the man who had received his sight, 19and asked them, "Is this your son, who you say was born blind? How then does he now see?" 20His parents answered, "We know that this is our son, and that he was born blind; 21but how he now sees we do not know, nor do we know who opened his eyes. Ask him; he is of age, he will speak for himself." 22His parents said this because they feared the Jews, for the Jews had already agreed that if any one should confess him to be Christ, he was to be put out of the synagogue. 23Therefore his parents said, "He is of age, ask him."

24So for the second time they called the man who had been blind, and said to him, "Give God the praise; we know that this man is a sinner." 25He answered, "Whether he is a sinner, I do not know; one thing I know, that though I was blind, now I see." 26They said to him, "What did he do to you? How did he open your eyes?" 27He answered them, "I have told you already, and you would not listen. Why do you want to hear it again? Do you too want to become his disciples?" 28And they reviled him, saying, "You are his disciple, but we are disciples of Moses. 29We know that God has spoken to Moses, but as for this man, we do not know where he comes from." 30The man answered, "Why, this is a marvel! You do not know where he comes from, and yet he opened my eyes. [31]We know that God does not listen to sinners, but if any one is a worshiper of God and does his will, God listens to him. [32]Never since the world began has it been heard that any one opened the eyes of a man born blind. [33]If this man were not from God, he could do nothing." [34]They answered him, "You were born in utter sin, and would you teach us?" And they cast him out.

REFLECTIONS FROM THE CHURCH FATHERS

A Failed Attempt to Nullify the Miracle, CHRYSOSTOM. It is the nature of truth to be strengthened by the very snares that are laid against it by people. . . . Lies defeat themselves by the very means they use against the truth, making it appear even brighter, as is the case now. For the argument that might otherwise have been urged—that is, that the neighbors knew nothing for certain but were guessing on the basis that this man looked like the one who was healed—that whole argument is cut off by the introduction of the parents who could, of course, testify to their own son. The Pharisees, being unable by intimidation to deter the blind man from publicly proclaiming his benefactor, try to nullify the miracle through the parents. *Homilies on the Gospel of John 58.1.*

The Facts Prove Jesus Is Not a Sinner, THEODORE OF MOPSUESTIA. So Jesus must be admired, the blind man says, as one who is superior to human thought. While you do not know where he is from, the accomplished miracle openly proves his power to me. You do not know who he is and would need testimony from others if there had been no clue of his power. But if his miracles show that he is a great man—and you still do not know where he is from or who he is—it is evident, both from the greatness of his miracles and your foolishness, that he is beyond human comprehension. And from these facts it seems clear that he cannot be called a sinner. Certainly God does not fulfill the requests of sinners but listens instead to the voice of those who show honest behavior and faithfully do his will. . . . Indeed, he healed a man born blind, and we know that this has never been done before, not even by Moses, whom you admire. *Commentary on John 4.9.30-32.*

CLOSING PRAYER

Lord, we implore you, grant your people grace to withstand the temptations of the world, the flesh and the devil, and with pure hearts and minds to follow you, the only God, through Jesus Christ our Lord. Amen. *Gelasian Sacramentary*

FURTHER READING: Psalm 118; 145

MONDAY

Jesus said, "If anyone would come after me, let him deny himself and take up his cross and follow me." (Mark 8:34 BCP)

CONFESSION: See page 11.

SCRIPTURE READING: John 9:34-41

[34]They answered him, "You were born in utter sin, and would you teach us?" And they cast him out.

[35]Jesus heard that they had cast him out, and having found him he said, "Do you believe in the Son of man?" [36]He answered, "And who is he, sir, that I may believe in him?" [37]Jesus said to him, "You have seen him, and it is he who speaks to you." [38]He said, "Lord, I

believe"; and he worshiped him. [39]Jesus said, "For judgment I came into this world, that those who do not see may see, and that those who see may become blind." [40]Some of the Pharisees near him heard this, and they said to him, "Are we also blind?" [41]Jesus said to them, "If you were blind, you would have no guilt; but now that you say, 'We see,' your guilt remains."

REFLECTIONS FROM THE CHURCH FATHERS

Worship Follows Faith, BASIL THE GREAT. Worship follows faith, and faith is confirmed by power. But if you say that believers also know, they know from what they believe; and vice versa, they believe from what they know. We know God from his power. We, therefore, believe in him who is known, and we worship him who is believed. *Letter 234.3.*

Light and Darkness, Seeing and Blind, AUGUSTINE. The day then was divided between light and darkness. . . . And this is only right since you, O Lord, are the light, you are the day, you deliver us from darkness. Every soul accepts and understands this. But what is this that follows, "And those who see may become blind"? Because you have arrived, shall those who saw now be made blind? Hear what comes next, and maybe you will understand. "Some of the Pharisees" were disturbed by these words "and said to him, 'Are we also blind?'" What had moved them were the words "And those who see may become blind." "Jesus said to them, . . . 'If you were blind, you would have no sin,'" that is, if you identified yourselves as blind you would run to the physician. . . . For I have come to take away sin. But now you say, "We see." Therefore your sin remains. Why? Because when you say that you see, you are not looking for a physician, and that is why you will remain in your blindness. *Tractates on the Gospel of John 44.16-17.*

CLOSING PRAYER

O God, you divide the day from the night; separate our deeds from the darkness of sin, that we may continually live in your light, and reflect in all our deeds your eternal beauty. Amen. *Leonine Sacramentary*

FURTHER READING: Psalm 31; 35

TUESDAY

Jesus said, "If anyone would come after me, let him deny himself and take up his cross and follow me." (Mark 8:34 BCP)

CONFESSION: See page 11.

SCRIPTURE READING: John 10:1-18

[1]"Truly, truly, I say to you, he who does not enter the sheepfold by the door but climbs in by another way, that man is a thief and a robber; [2]but he who enters by the door is the shepherd of the sheep. [3]To him the gatekeeper opens; the sheep hear his voice, and he calls his own sheep by name and leads them out. [4]When he has brought out all his own, he goes before them, and the sheep follow him, for they know his voice. [5]A stranger they will not follow, but they will flee from him, for they do not know the voice of strangers." [6]This figure Jesus used with them, but they did not understand what he was saying to them.

[7]So Jesus again said to them, "Truly, truly, I say to you, I am the door of the sheep. [8]All who came before me are thieves and robbers; but the sheep did not heed them. [9]I am the door; if any one enters by

me, he will be saved, and will go in and out and find pasture. ¹⁰The thief comes only to steal and kill and destroy; I came that they may have life, and have it abundantly. ¹¹I am the good shepherd. The good shepherd lays down his life for the sheep. ¹²He who is a hireling and not a shepherd, whose own the sheep are not, sees the wolf coming and leaves the sheep and flees; and the wolf snatches them and scatters them. ¹³He flees because he is a hireling and cares nothing for the sheep. ¹⁴I am the good shepherd; I know my own and my own know me, ¹⁵as the Father knows me and I know the Father; and I lay down my life for the sheep. ¹⁶And I have other sheep, that are not of this fold; I must bring them also, and they will heed my voice. So there shall be one flock, one shepherd. ¹⁷For this reason the Father loves me, because I lay down my life, that I may take it again. ¹⁸No one takes it from me, but I lay it down of my own accord. I have power to lay it down, and I have power to take it again; this charge I have received from my Father."

REFLECTIONS FROM THE CHURCH FATHERS

Bringing in the Sheep, PETER CHRYSOLOGUS. Each year, when spring with its breezes begins to usher in the birth of so many sheep and to deposit the numerous young of the fruitful flock about the fields, the meadows and the paths, a good shepherd puts aside his songs and leisure. He anxiously searches for the tender little sheep, picks them up and gathers them together. Happy to carry them, he places them about his neck, on his shoulders and in his arms. He wants them to be safe as he carries or leads them to the protecting sheepfolds.

That is the case with ourselves, too. When we see our ecclesiastical flock gaining rich increase under the favoring smile of the spring of Lent, we put aside the resonant tones of our treatise and the customary fare of our discourse. Concerned about our very heavy labor, we give all our concern to gathering and carrying in the heavenly [lambs]. *Sermon 40.*

Sheep Need a Shepherd, CLEMENT OF ALEXANDRIA. In our sickness we need a Savior, in our wanderings a guide, in our blindness someone to show us the light, in our thirst the fountain of living water that quenches forever the thirst of those who drink from it. We dead people need life, we sheep need a shepherd, we children need a teacher, the whole world needs Jesus! *Christ the Educator 1.9.83.*

CLOSING PRAYER

O Sovereign and Almighty Lord, bless all your people and all your flock. Give peace, your help, your love unto us, your servants, the sheep of your fold, that we may be united in the bond of peace and love, one body and one spirit, in one hope of our calling, in your Divine and boundless love; for the sake of Jesus Christ, the great Shepherd of the sheep. Amen. *Liturgy of St. Mark*

FURTHER READING: Psalm 120–127

WEDNESDAY

†

Jesus said, "If anyone would come after me, let him deny himself and take up his cross and follow me." (Mark 8:34 BCP)

CONFESSION: See page 11.

SCRIPTURE READING: John 10:19-42

[19]There was again a division among the Jews because of these words. [20]Many of them said, "He has a demon, and he is mad; why

listen to him?" ²¹Others said, "These are not the sayings of one who has a demon. Can a demon open the eyes of the blind?"

²²It was the feast of the Dedication at Jerusalem; ²³it was winter, and Jesus was walking in the temple, in the portico of Solomon. ²⁴So the Jews gathered round him and said to him, "How long will you keep us in suspense? If you are the Christ, tell us plainly." ²⁵Jesus answered them, "I told you, and you do not believe. The works that I do in my Father's name, they bear witness to me; ²⁶but you do not believe, because you do not belong to my sheep. ²⁷My sheep hear my voice, and I know them, and they follow me; ²⁸and I give them eternal life, and they shall never perish, and no one shall snatch them out of my hand. ²⁹My Father, who has given them to me, is greater than all, and no one is able to snatch them out of the Father's hand. ³⁰I and the Father are one."

³¹The Jews took up stones again to stone him. ³²Jesus answered them, "I have shown you many good works from the Father; for which of these do you stone me?" ³³The Jews answered him, "It is not for a good work that we stone you but for blasphemy; because you, being a man, make yourself God." ³⁴Jesus answered them, "Is it not written in your law, 'I said, you are gods'? ³⁵If he called them gods to whom the word of God came (and scripture cannot be broken), ³⁶do you say of him whom the Father consecrated and sent into the world, 'You are blaspheming,' because I said, 'I am the Son of God'? ³⁷If I am not doing the works of my Father, then do not believe me; ³⁸but if I do them, even though you do not believe me, believe the works, that you may know and understand that the Father is in me and I am in the Father." ³⁹Again they tried to arrest him, but he escaped from their hands.

⁴⁰He went away again across the Jordan to the place where John at first baptized, and there he remained. ⁴¹And many came to him; and they said, "John did no sign, but everything that John said about this man was true." ⁴²And many believed in him there.

REFLECTIONS FROM THE CHURCH FATHERS

Christ, Who Is Life, Gives Life, CYRIL OF ALEXANDRIA. Christ promises his followers eternal life as a compensation and reward. They receive exemption from death and corruption and from the torments the judge inflicts upon transgressors. By giving life, Christ shows that by nature he *is* life. He does not receive it from another but supplies it from his own resources. And by eternal life we understand not only length of days which all, both good and bad, shall possess after the resurrection but also the passing of those days in bliss.

It is also possible to understand by "life" a reference to the mystical blessing [of the Eucharist] by which Christ implants in us his own life through the participation of his own flesh by the faithful, according to the text, "He who eats my flesh and drinks my blood has eternal life." *Commentary on the Gospel of John 7.1.*

An Equal in an Equal, AUGUSTINE. The Son does not say, "The Father is in me, and I in him," in the sense in which we say it. For if our thinking is in line with him, then we are in God. And if we live the way he wants us to, then God is in us. Believers, by participating in his grace and being illuminated by him, are said to be in him and he in us. But this is not how it is with the only begotten Son. He is in the Father, and the Father is in him as one who is equal is in him whose equal he is. In short, we can sometimes say, "We are in God, and God is in us," but can we say I and God are one? You are in God because God contains you. God is in you because you have become the temple of God. . . . Recognize the prerogative of the Lord and the privilege of the servant. The prerogative of the Lord is equality with the Father; the privilege of the servant is fellowship with the Savior. *Tractates on the Gospel of John 48.10.*

CLOSING PRAYER

As each day passes, the end of my life becomes ever nearer, and my sins increase in number. You, Lord, my Creator, know how feeble I am, and in my weakness, strengthen me; when I suffer, uphold me, and I will glorify you, my Lord and my God. *Ephraem of Syria*

FURTHER READING: Psalm 119:145-176; 128–130

THURSDAY

✝

Jesus said, "If anyone would come after me, let him deny himself and take up his cross and follow me." (Mark 8:34 BCP)

CONFESSION: See page 11.

SCRIPTURE READING: John 11:1-27

[1]Now a certain man was ill, Lazarus of Bethany, the village of Mary and her sister Martha. [2]It was Mary who anointed the Lord with ointment and wiped his feet with her hair, whose brother Lazarus was ill. [3]So the sisters sent to him, saying, "Lord, he whom you love is ill." [4]But when Jesus heard it he said, "This illness is not unto death; it is for the glory of God, so that the Son of God may be glorified by means of it."

[5]Now Jesus loved Martha and her sister and Lazarus. [6]So when he heard that he was ill, he stayed two days longer in the place where he was. [7]Then after this he said to the disciples, "Let us go into Judea again." [8]The disciples said to him, "Rabbi, the Jews were but now seeking to stone you, and are you going there again?" [9]Jesus

answered, "Are there not twelve hours in the day? If any one walks in the day, he does not stumble, because he sees the light of this world. [10]But if any one walks in the night, he stumbles, because the light is not in him." [11]Thus he spoke, and then he said to them, "Our friend Lazarus has fallen asleep, but I go to awake him out of sleep." [12]The disciples said to him, "Lord, if he has fallen asleep, he will recover." [13]Now Jesus had spoken of his death, but they thought that he meant taking rest in sleep. [14]Then Jesus told them plainly, "Lazarus is dead; [15]and for your sake I am glad that I was not there, so that you may believe. But let us go to him." [16]Thomas, called the Twin, said to his fellow disciples, "Let us also go, that we may die with him."

[17]Now when Jesus came, he found that Lazarus had already been in the tomb four days. [18]Bethany was near Jerusalem, about two miles off, [19]and many of the Jews had come to Martha and Mary to console them concerning their brother. [20]When Martha heard that Jesus was coming, she went and met him, while Mary sat in the house. [21]Martha said to Jesus, "Lord, if you had been here, my brother would not have died. [22]And even now I know that whatever you ask from God, God will give you." [23]Jesus said to her, "Your brother will rise again." [24]Martha said to him, "I know that he will rise again in the resurrection at the last day." [25]Jesus said to her, "I am the resurrection and the life; he who believes in me, though he die, yet shall he live, [26]and whoever lives and believes in me shall never die. Do you believe this?" [27]She said to him, "Yes, Lord; I believe that you are the Christ, the Son of God, he who is coming into the world."

REFLECTIONS FROM THE CHURCH FATHERS

Stumbling Without the Light of Christ, ATHANASIUS. Consider what I have said, that the Light is Christ. Everyone who will walk in his commandments will not be laid hold of by evil. These twelve hours that are in the day are the twelve apostles. The devil . . . is compared with the night. He who walks in the will of the devil will stumble because he does not have the light of Christ. *Homily on the Resurrection of Lazarus.*

Christ As Pledge of our Resurrection Foreshadowed in Old Testament, APOSTOLIC CONSTITUTIONS. For the almighty God himself will raise us up through our Lord Jesus Christ, according to his infallible promise, and grant us a resurrection with all those that have slept from the beginning of the world. And we shall then be such as we now are in our present form, without any defect or corruption. For we shall rise incorruptible: whether we die at sea, or are scattered on the earth or are torn to pieces by wild beasts and birds, he will raise us by his own power. For the whole world is held together by the hand of God. *Constitutions of the Holy Apostles 5.1.7.*

CLOSING PRAYER

When the dawn appears, when the light grows, when midday burns, when the holy light has ended, when the clear night comes; I sing your praises, O Father, healer of hearts, healer of bodies, giver of wisdom, remedy of evil, O Giver also of a life without evil, A life not troubled by earthly fear— . . . keep my heart in purity, let my songs speak of the hidden source of created things; and, far from God, never let me be drawn into sin. *Synesius*

FURTHER READING: Psalm 131–133; 142; 149

FRIDAY

†

Jesus said, "If anyone would come after me, let him deny himself and take up his cross and follow me." (Mark 8:34 BCP)

CONFESSION: See page 11.

SCRIPTURE READING: John 11:28-44

²⁸When she had said this, she went and called her sister Mary, saying quietly, "The Teacher is here and is calling for you." ²⁹And when she heard it, she rose quickly and went to him. ³⁰Now Jesus had not yet come to the village, but was still in the place where Martha had met him. ³¹When the Jews who were with her in the house, consoling her, saw Mary rise quickly and go out, they followed her, supposing that she was going to the tomb to weep there. ³²Then Mary, when she came where Jesus was and saw him, fell at his feet, saying to him, "Lord, if you had been here, my brother would not have died." ³³When Jesus saw her weeping, and the Jews who came with her also weeping, he was deeply moved in spirit and troubled; ³⁴and he said, "Where have you laid him?" They said to him, "Lord, come and see." ³⁵Jesus wept. ³⁶So the Jews said, "See how he loved him!" ³⁷But some of them said, "Could not he who opened the eyes of the blind man have kept this man from dying?"

³⁸Then Jesus, deeply moved again, came to the tomb; it was a cave, and a stone lay upon it. ³⁹Jesus said, "Take away the stone." Martha, the sister of the dead man, said to him, "Lord, by this time there will be an odor, for he has been dead four days." ⁴⁰Jesus said to her, "Did I not tell you that if you would believe you would see the glory of God?" ⁴¹So they took away the stone. And Jesus lifted

up his eyes and said, "Father, I thank thee that thou hast heard me. [42]I knew that you hear me always, but I have said this on account of the people standing by, that they may believe that thou didst send me." [43]When he had said this, he cried with a loud voice, "Lazarus, come out." [44]The dead man came out, his hands and feet bound with bandages, and his face wrapped with a cloth. Jesus said to them, "Unbind him, and let him go."

REFLECTIONS FROM THE CHURCH FATHERS

God Wept, Moved by Mortals' Tears, POTAMIUS OF LISBON. God wept, moved by the tears of mortals, and although he was about to release Lazarus from the bond of death by the exercise of his power, he fulfilled the component of human affection with the comfort of his sympathetic tears. God wept, not because he learned that the young man had died before him but in order to moderate the sisters' outpourings of grief. God wept, in order that God might do, with tears and compassion, what human beings do on behalf of their fellow human beings. God wept, because human nature had fallen to such an extent that, after being expelled from eternity, it had come to love the lower world. God wept, because those who could be immortal, the devil made mortal. God wept, because those whom he had rewarded with every benefit and had placed under his power, those whom he had set in paradise, among flowers and lilies without any hardship, the devil, by teaching them to sin, exiled from almost every delight. God wept, because those whom he had created innocent, the devil through his wickedness, caused to be found guilty. *On Lazarus.*

The Sweet Odor of Paradise Invades the Stench of Death, ATHANASIUS. "Come forth." See, I am standing by you. I am your Lord. You are the work of my hands. Why have you not known me, because in the beginning I myself formed Adam from the earth and gave him breath? Open your mouth yourself so that I may give you breath. Stand on your feet and receive strength for yourself. For I am the strength of the whole creation. Stretch out your hands, and I shall give them strength. For I am the straight staff. I command the foul odor to depart from you. For I am the sweet odor of the trees of paradise. Behold, the prophecy of Isaiah the prophet will be fulfilled in you, namely, "I shall open your tombs, and I shall bring you forth." *Homily on the Resurrection of Lazarus.*

CLOSING PRAYER

Let us pray to the Lord without duplicity, in tune with one another, entreating him with sighs and tears, as befits people in our position—placed as we are between the many, lamenting that they have fallen away, and the faithful remnant that fears it may do the same itself; between the weak, laid low in large number, and the few still standing firm. Let us pray that peace may very soon be restored to us, help reach us in our dangers, to draw us from our dark retreats, and let God's gracious promises to his servants find fulfillment. May we see the Church restored and our salvation secured; after the rain, fair weather; after the darkness, light; after these storms and tempests, a gentle calm. Let us ask him to help us, because he loves us as a father loves his children, and to give us the tokens of his divine power that are usual with him. So will our persecutors be stopped from blaspheming, those who have fallen away repent to some purpose, and the firm, unwavering faith of the steadfast be crowned with glory. *Cyprian of Carthage*

FURTHER READING: Psalm 22; 95; 141; 143

Saturday

✝

Jesus said, "If anyone would come after me, let him deny himself and take up his cross and follow me." (Mark 8:34 BCP)

Confession: See page 11.

Scripture Reading: John 12:1-8

¹Six days before the Passover, Jesus came to Bethany, where Lazarus was, whom Jesus had raised from the dead. ²There they made him a supper; Martha served, and Lazarus was one of those at table with him. ³Mary took a pound of costly ointment of pure nard and anointed the feet of Jesus and wiped his feet with her hair; and the house was filled with the fragrance of the ointment. ⁴But Judas Iscariot, one of his disciples (he who was to betray him), said, ⁵"Why was this ointment not sold for three hundred denarii and given to the poor?" ⁶This he said, not that he cared for the poor but because he was a thief, and as he had the money box he used to take what was put into it. ⁷Jesus said, "Let her alone, let her keep it for the day of my burial. ⁸The poor you always have with you, but you do not always have me."

Reflections from the Church Fathers

Pouring Ointment on Jesus' Feet, Ambrose. In loving this body, that is, the church, bring water for his feet and kiss his feet, not only pardoning those who have become enmeshed in sin but by your peace giving them harmony and putting them at peace. Pour ointment on his feet, that the whole house wherein Christ reclines at table may be filled with the odor of your ointment, that all at table with him may be pleased with your perfume. In other words, pay honor to the least. *Letter 62 (to his sister).*

Abundance of Oil Covers Abundance of Sin, EPHREM THE SYRIAN.

An abundance is oil with which sinners do business: the forgiveness of sins.

By oil the Anointed forgave the sins of the sinner who anointed [his] feet.

With [oil] Mary poured out her sin upon the head of the Lord of her sins.

It wafted its scent; it tested the reclining as in a furnace:

It exposed the theft clothed in the care of the poor.

It became the bridge to the remembrance of Mary to pass on her glory from generation to generation.

In its flowings is hidden joy, for oil does indeed gladden the face.

It brings its shoulder to all burdens in rejoicing and grieving with everyone:

For it serves joy yet is obeyed by gloom,

For faces joyful of life by it are resplendent,

And with it, the gloomy face of death is prepared for burial and dies.

Hymns on Virginity 4.11-12.

CLOSING PRAYER

Shed forth, O Lord, we pray your light into our hearts, that we may perceive the light of your commandments, and walking in your way may fall into no error; through Jesus Christ our Lord. Amen. *Gelasian Sacramentary*

FURTHER READING: Psalm 42; 43; 137; 144

Week Six

Almighty and everliving God, in your tender love for the human race you sent your Son our Savior Jesus Christ to take upon him our nature, and to suffer death upon the cross, giving us the example of his great humility: Mercifully grant that we may walk in the way of his suffering, and also share in his resurrection; through Jesus Christ our Lord, who lives and reigns with you and the Holy Spirit, one God, for ever and ever. *Amen.* COLLECT FOR THE SUNDAY OF THE PASSION.

SUNDAY

†

"All we like sheep have gone astray; we have turned every one to his own way; and the Lord has laid on him the iniquity of us all." (Isaiah 53:6 BCP)

CONFESSION: See page 11.

SCRIPTURE READING: John 12:9-19

⁹When the great crowd of the Jews learned that he was there, they came, not only on account of Jesus but also to see Lazarus, whom he had raised from the dead. ¹⁰So the chief priests planned to put Lazarus also to death, ¹¹because on account of him many of the Jews were going away and believing in Jesus.

¹²The next day a great crowd who had come to the feast heard that Jesus was coming to Jerusalem. ¹³So they took branches of palm trees and went out to meet him, crying, "Hosanna! Blessed is he who comes in the name of the Lord, even the King of Israel!" ¹⁴And Jesus found a young ass and sat upon it; as it is written,

¹⁵"Fear not, daughter of Zion;
   behold, your king is coming,
   sitting on an ass's colt!"

¹⁶His disciples did not understand this at first; but when Jesus was glorified, then they remembered that this had been written of him and had been done to him. ¹⁷The crowd that had been with him when he called Lazarus out of the tomb and raised him from the dead bore witness. ¹⁸The reason why the crowd went to meet him was that they heard he had done this sign. ¹⁹The Pharisees then said to one another, "You see that you can do nothing; look, the world has gone after him."

Reflections from the Church Fathers

The Crowd Knows Better Than Their Leaders, CHRYSOSTOM. Wealth is just as liable as power to destroy those who are not careful. The first leads into covetousness; the second, into pride. See, for instance, how the multitude of the Jews is sound while their rulers are corrupt. For the first of these believed Christ, as the Evangelists continually assert, saying that "many of the multitude believed on him," but those who were of the ruling party did not believe. . . . But how is it that he now enters openly into Jerusalem whereas before he had not walked openly among the Jews and had withdrawn into the wilderness? Having quenched their anger by withdrawing, he comes to them now when they are calmer. Moreover, the multitude that went before him and then followed after him was enough to throw them into an agony of fear. For no miracle so attracted the people as that of Lazarus. And another Evangelist says that they threw their garments under his feet and that "the whole city was moved." This is the kind of honor he had when he entered the city. *Homilies on the Gospel of John 66.1.*

Palms of Victory over Death, ROMANUS MELODUS.
With palms everyone came
On the occasion of your arrival, Savior,
Crying to you, "Hosanna!"
Now all of us sing praises to you
From our pitiful mouths,
As we wave to you the branches of our souls and cry out:
"O you, who are in the highest, save the world
That you brought into being, Lord,
And blot out our sins,
Just as you previously dried
The tears of Mary and Martha."
The holy church holds a high festival,

Faithfully calling together her children,
O Lover of humanity;
With palms she meets you and strews garments of joy
So that you, along with your disciples and your friends,
May establish your feet and grant deep peace for your servants,
And release them from oppression, as previously you checked
The tears of Mary and Martha.
Incline your ear, O God of the universe,
And hear our prayers,
And snatch us from the bonds of death. . . .
Let those of us who have died because of our sins, and who dwell
     in the tomb
Because of our knowledge of evils,
Imitate the sisters of faithful Lazarus as we cry to Christ with
     tears, and in faith and in love:
"Save us, you who willed to become man.
And raise us up from the tomb of our sins,
You, alone who are immortal."
Kontakion on the Raising of Lazarus 27.14-17.

Closing Prayer

I bind unto myself today
The strong name of the Trinity,
By invocation of the same,
The Three in One, and One in Three.

I bind this day to me for ever,
By power of faith, Christ's incarnation,
His baptism in the Jordan River,
His death on the cross for my salvation,
His bursting from the spiced tomb,
His riding up the heavenly way,
His coming at the day of doom,

I bind unto myself today . . .

. . . I bind unto myself today
Your power, O God, to hold and lead,
Your eye to watch, your might to stay,
Your ear to hearken to my need,
Your wisdom, O my God, to teach,
Your hand to guide, your shield to ward,
Your living Word to give me speech,
Your heavenly host to be my guard.

I bind unto myself the Name,
The strong name of the Trinity,
By invocation of the same,
The Three in One, and One in Three.
St. Patrick

FURTHER READING: Psalm 24; 29; 103

MONDAY

"All we like sheep have gone astray; we have turned every one to his own way; and the Lord has laid on him the iniquity of us all." (Isaiah 53:6 BCP)

CONFESSION: See page 11.

SCRIPTURE READING: John 12:20-26

[20]Now among those who went up to worship at the feast were some Greeks. [21]So these came to Philip, who was from Bethsaida in Galilee, and said to him, "Sir, we wish to see Jesus." [22]Philip went and told Andrew; Andrew went with Philip and they told Jesus. [23]And Jesus answered them, "The hour has come for the Son of man to be glorified. [24]Truly, truly, I say to you, unless a grain of wheat falls into the earth and dies, it remains alone; but if it dies, it bears much fruit. [25]He who loves his life loses it, and he who hates his life in this world will keep it for eternal life. [26]If any one serves me, he must follow me; and where I am, there shall my servant be also; if any one serves me, the Father will honor him."

REFLECTIONS FROM THE CHURCH FATHERS

When You Love Yourself, AUGUSTINE. There is not anyone, after all, who does not love himself. But we have to look for the right sort of love and avoid the wrong sort. You see, anyone who loves himself by leaving God out of his life (and leaves God out of his life by loving himself), does not even remain *in* himself. He actually leaves his self. He goes away into exile from his own heart by taking no notice of what is inside and instead only loving what is outside. . . . For instance, let me ask you this: Are you money? . . . And yet, by loving money, you end up abandoning yourself. First you abandon and then later end up destroying yourself. Love of money, you see, has caused you to destroy yourself. You tell lies on account of money. . . . While looking for money, you have destroyed your soul. . . .

Come back to yourself. But then turn upward when you have come back to yourself; do not stay in yourself. First come back to yourself from the things outside you, and then give yourself back to the one who made you, who looked for you when you were lost and found you when you were a runaway. *Sermon 330.2-3.*

The Path to Divine Glory Leads to God, CYRIL OF ALEXANDRIA. Since the author of our salvation did not travel by the path of glory and luxury but by that of dishonor and hardships, we must do the same thing without complaining if we are to reach the same destination and share in the divine glory. But what honor shall we receive if we refuse to endure sufferings like those of our Master? . . . The one who does things pleasing to God serves Christ, but the one who follows his own wishes is a follower of himself and not of God. *Commentary on the Gospel of John 8.*

CLOSING PRAYER

Almighty and everliving God, in your tender love for the human race you sent your Son our Savior Jesus Christ to take upon him our nature, and to suffer death upon the cross, giving us the example of his great humility: Mercifully grant that we may walk in the way of his suffering, and also share in his resurrection; through Jesus Christ our Lord, who lives and reigns with you and the Holy Spirit, one God, for ever and ever. Amen. *Gregorian Sacramentary*

FURTHER READING: Psalm 51; 69:1-23

TUESDAY

"All we like sheep have gone astray; we have turned every one to his own way; and the Lord has laid on him the iniquity of us all." (Isaiah 53:6 BCP)

CONFESSION: See page 11.

SCRIPTURE READING: John 12:27-36

[27]"Now is my soul troubled. And what shall I say? 'Father, save me from this hour'? No, for this purpose I have come to this hour. [28]Father, glorify thy name." Then a voice came from heaven, "I have glorified it, and I will glorify it again." [29]The crowd standing by heard it and said that it had thundered. Others said, "An angel has spoken to him." [30]Jesus answered, "This voice has come for your sake, not for mine. [31]Now is the judgment of this world, now shall the ruler of this world be cast out; [32]and I, when I am lifted up from the earth, will draw all men to myself." [33]He said this to show by what death he was to die. [34]The crowd answered him, "We have heard from the law that the Christ remains for ever. How can you say that the Son of man must be lifted up? Who is this Son of man?" [35]Jesus said to them, "The light is with you for a little longer. Walk while you have the light, lest the darkness over-take you; he who walks in the darkness does not know where he goes. [36]While you have the light, believe in the light, that you may become sons of light."

When Jesus had said this, he departed and hid himself from them.

REFLECTIONS FROM THE CHURCH FATHERS

His Suffering Strengthens Us, AUGUSTINE. I heard him saying pre-viously . . . "If anyone wants to serve me, let him follow me. And where I am, there my servant shall also be." And so, I was all on fire to despise the world, and the whole of this life, however long it might be, had become only a vapor before my eyes. In compari-son with my love for eternal things, everything temporal had lost its value for me. But now, this same Lord, whose words had trans-ported me from the weakness that was mine to the strength that was his—I now hear him saying, "How is my soul troubled." What does this mean? How can you ask my soul to follow you when I see your own in so much turmoil? How can I endure when even a strength as great as yours feels it is a heavy burden? What kind of foundation am I left with when the Rock is giving way? But the Lord is already forming the answer inside my own head, saying: You shall follow me that much better, because it is to strengthen your own endurance that I included this. You have heard, as if addressed to yourself, the voice of my strength. Now hear in me the voice of your infirmity. I supply strength when you need to run without slowing you down, but I take on myself whatever makes you afraid, paving the way for you to continue your march. Lord, I acknowledge your mercy! You, who are so great, allowed yourself to be troubled in order to console all of those in your body who are troubled by the continual experience of their own weakness—keeping them from perishing utterly in despair. *Tractates on the Gospel of John 52.2.*

Christ's Human Nature Had to Feel What We Feel, Cyril of Alexandria. Only the death of the Savior could bring an end to death, and it is the same for each of the other sufferings of the flesh too. Unless he had felt dread, human nature could not have become free from dread. Unless he had experienced grief, there could have never been any deliverance from grief. Unless he had been troubled and alarmed, there would have been no escape from these feelings. Every one of the emotions to which human nature is liable can be found in Christ. The emotions of his flesh were aroused, not that they might gain the upper hand, as indeed they do in us, but in order that when aroused they might be thoroughly subdued by the power of the Word dwelling in the flesh, human nature as a whole thus undergoing a change for the better. *Commentary on the Gospel of John 8.*

Closing Prayer

God's compassion for us is all the more wonderful because Christ died not for the righteous or the holy but for the wicked and the sinful, and, though the divine nature could not be touched by the sting of death, he took to himself, through his birth as one of us, something he could offer on our behalf. *Leo the Great*

FURTHER READING: Psalm 6; 12; 94

WEDNESDAY
✝

"All we like sheep have gone astray; we have turned every one to his own way; and the Lord has laid on him the iniquity of us all." (Isaiah 53:6 BCP)

CONFESSION: See page 11.

SCRIPTURE READING: John 12:37-50

[37]Though he had done so many signs before them, yet they did not believe in him; [38]it was that the word spoken by the prophet Isaiah might be fulfilled:

> "Lord, who has believed our report,
> and to whom has the arm of the Lord been revealed?"

[39]Therefore they could not believe. For Isaiah again said,

> [40]"He has blinded their eyes and hardened their heart, lest they should see with their eyes and perceive with their heart, and turn for me to heal them."

[41]Isaiah said this because he saw his glory and spoke of him. [42]Nevertheless many even of the authorities believed in him, but

for fear of the Pharisees they did not confess it, lest they should be put out of the synagogue: [43]for they loved the praise of men more than the praise of God.

[44]And Jesus cried out and said, "He who believes in me, believes not in me but in him who sent me. [45]And he who sees me sees him who sent me. [46]I have come as light into the world, that whoever believes in me may not remain in darkness. [47]If any one hears my sayings and does not keep them, I do not judge him; for I did not come to judge the world but to save the world. [48]He who rejects me and does not receive my sayings has a judge; the word that I have spoken will be his judge on the last day. [49]For I have not spoken on my own authority; the Father who sent me has himself given me commandment what to say and what to speak. [50]And I know that his commandment is eternal life. What I say, therefore, I say as the Father has bidden me."

Reflections from the Church Fathers

Blinded by Pride, Augustine. It is no wonder, then, that they could not believe when such was their pride of will, that, being ignorant of the righteousness of God, they wished to establish their own [righteousness]. As the apostle says of them, "They have not submitted themselves to the righteousness of God." For it was not by faith, but as it were by works, that they were puffed up. And blinded by this very self-elation, they stumbled against the stone of stumbling. And so it is said, "They could not," by which we are to understand that they would not. . . .

See, I also say, that those who have such lofty ideas of themselves as to suppose that so much must be attributed to the powers of their own will, that they deny their need of the divine assistance in order to attain to a righteous life, cannot believe on Christ. For the mere syllables of Christ's name and the Christian sacraments are of no profit where faith in Christ is itself resisted. For faith in Christ is to believe in him that justifies the ungodly. It means to believe in the Mediator, without whose intervention we cannot be reconciled to God. It means to believe in the Savior who came to seek and to save that which was lost, to believe in him who said, "Without me you can do nothing." *Tractates on the Gospel of John 53.9-10.*

The True Light Shines in the Darkness, ORIGEN. When the Savior of the world came, he made the true light shine. But they did not want to gaze on it, nor were they willing to walk by the radiance of his teaching. Consequently, darkness overtook them and demanded a penalty for the wickedness that had preoccupied them. And this [darkness] might be said to have reasonably blinded and hardened them. And, just as it follows that the one who has chosen to walk in the light also knows where he is going, so it follows that the one who has not chosen to walk in the light walks in darkness and travels wretchedly along the road of the blind. . . .

For just as the visible sun shoots out its bright beams in order to enlighten those who have ailing eyes, so also does the spiritual Sun, the Light that has no setting or evening, come to the world and through his divine and ineffable miracles cast the brilliant gleam of his deity far and wide. *Fragment 94 on the Gospel of John.*

CLOSING PRAYER

Lord, I pray that you may be a lamp for me in the darkness. Touch my soul and kindle a fire within it, that it may burn brightly and give light to my life. Thus my body may truly become your temple, lit by your perpetual flame burning on the altar of my heart. And may the light within me shine on my brothers and sisters that it may drive away the darkness of ignorance and sin from them also. Thus let us be lights to the world, manifesting the bright beauty of your gospel to all around us. *Columbanus*

FURTHER READING: Psalm 55; 74

THURSDAY

✝

"All we like sheep have gone astray; we have turned every one to his own way; and the Lord has laid on him the iniquity of us all." (Isaiah 53:6 BCP)

CONFESSION: See page 11.

SCRIPTURE READING: John 17:1-11

[1]When Jesus had spoken these words, he lifted up his eyes to heaven and said, "Father, the hour has come; glorify thy Son that the Son may glorify thee, [2]since thou hast given him power over all flesh, to give eternal life to all whom thou hast given him. [3]And this is eternal life, that they know thee the only true God, and Jesus Christ whom thou hast sent. [4]I glorified thee on earth, having accomplished the work which thou gave me to do; [5]and now, Father, glorify thou me in thy own presence with the glory which I had with thee before the world was made.

[6]"I have manifested thy name to the men whom thou gave me out of the world; yours they were, and thou gave them to me, and they have kept thy word. [7]Now they know that everything that thou hast given me is from thee; [8]for I have given them the words which thou gave me, and they have received them and know in truth that I came from thee; and they have believed that thou didst send me. [9]I am praying for them; I am not praying for the world but for

those whom thou hast given me, for they are yours; [10]all mine are yours, and yours are mine, and I am glorified in them. [11]And now I am no more in the world, but they are in the world, and I am coming to thee. Holy Father, keep them in thy name, which thou hast given me, that they may be one, even as we are one."

REFLECTIONS FROM THE CHURCH FATHERS

He Teaches How to Rely on the Father in Trials, CHRYSOSTOM. Christ not only speaks about the endurance of evil but puts himself forward as an example. After his admonition that "in the world you will have tribulation," he himself turns to prayer in order to teach us that in our testing we are to leave everything behind and flee to God. He had shaken their souls in his admonition but raised them up again by this prayer. *Homilies on the Gospel of John 80.1.*

Proved As Son by Nature, Not Adoption, HILARY OF POITIERS. He does not say that the day or the time but that the hour has come. An hour contains a portion of a day. What was this hour? . . . He was now to be spit on, scourged, crucified. But the Father glorifies the Son. The sun, instead of setting, fled, and all the other elements felt that same shock of the death of Christ. The stars in their courses, to avoid complicity in the crime, escaped by self-extinction from beholding the scene. The earth trembled under the weight of our Lord hanging on the cross and testified that it did not have the power to hold within it him who was dying. . . . The centurion proclaimed, "Truly this was the Son of God." Creation is set free by the mediation of this sin offering. The very rocks lose their solidity and strength. Those who had nailed him to the cross confess that truly this is the Son of God. The outcome justifies the assertion. Our Lord had said, "Glorify your Son," testifying that he was not the Son in name only but properly the Son. "Your Son," he said. Many of us are sons [children] of God. But he is Son in another sense. He is the proper, true Son by nature, not by adoption; in truth, not in name; by birth, not by creation. After he was glorified, that centurion's confession touched on the truth. And so, when the centurion confesses him to be the true Son of God, none of his believers might doubt what one of his persecutors could not deny. *On the Trinity 3.10-11.*

CLOSING PRAYER

O God, the strength of all those who put their trust in you, mercifully accept our prayers, and because through the weakness of our mortal nature we can do nothing good without you, grant us the help of your grace, that in keeping your commandments we may please you, both in will and deed, through Jesus Christ our Lord. Amen. *Gelasian Sacramentary*

FURTHER READING: Psalm 102; 142; 143

FRIDAY

✝

"All we like sheep have gone astray; we have turned every one to his own way; and the Lord has laid on him the iniquity of us all." (Isaiah 53:6 BCP)

CONFESSION: See page 11.

SCRIPTURE READING: John 19:16-24

[16]Then he handed him over to them to be crucified.

[17]So they took Jesus, and he went out, bearing his own cross, to the place called the place of a skull, which is called in Hebrew Golgotha. [18]There they crucified him, and with him two others, one on either side, and Jesus between them. [19]Pilate also wrote a title and put it on the cross; it read, "Jesus of Nazareth, the King of the Jews." [20]Many of the Jews read this title, for the place where Jesus was crucified was near the city; and it was written in Hebrew, in Latin, and in Greek. [21]The chief priests of the Jews then said to Pilate, "Do not write, 'The King of the Jews,' but, 'This man said, I am King of the Jews.'" [22]Pilate answered, "What I have written I have written."

[23]When the soldiers had crucified Jesus they took his garments and made four parts, one for each soldier; also his tunic. But the tunic was without seam, woven from top to bottom; [24]so they said to one another, "Let us not tear it, but cast lots for it to see whose it shall be." This was to fulfil the scripture, "They parted my garments among them, and for my clothing they cast lots."

REFLECTIONS FROM THE CHURCH FATHERS

He Became a Curse for Us, CYRIL OF ALEXANDRIA. They led away the author of life to die—to die for our sake. In a way beyond our understanding, the power of God brought from Christ's passion an end far different from that intended by his enemies. His sufferings served as a snare for death and rendered it powerless. The Lord's death proved to be our restoration to immortality and newness of life. Condemned to death though innocent, he went forward bearing on his shoulders the cross on which he was to suffer. He did this for our sake, taking on himself the punishment that the law justly imposed on sinners. He was cursed for our sake according to the saying of Scripture: "A curse is on everyone who is hanged on a tree." . . . We who have all committed many sins were under that ancient curse for our refusal to obey the law of God. To set us free he who was without sin took that curse on himself. Since he is God who is above all, his sufferings sufficed for all, his death in the flesh was the redemption of all. And so, Christ carried the cross, a cross that was rightfully not his but ours, who were under the condemnation of the law. . . . Indeed, our Lord Jesus Christ has warned us that anyone who does not take up his cross and follow him is not worthy of him. And I think taking up the cross means simply renouncing the world for God's sake and, if this is required of us, putting the hope of future blessings before the life we now live in the body. Our Lord Jesus Christ was not ashamed to carry the cross we deserved, and he did so because he loved us. *Commentary on the Gospel of John 12.*

The Cross Is the Scepter of Jesus' Power, LEO THE GREAT. When our Lord was handed over to the will of his cruel foes, they ordered him, in mockery of his royal dignity, to carry the instrument of his own torture. This was done to fulfill the prophecy of Isaiah: "A child is born for us, a son is given to us; sovereignty is laid on his shoulders."[18]To the wicked, the sight of the Lord carrying his own cross was indeed an object of derision. But to the faithful a great mystery was revealed, for the cross was destined to become the scepter of his power. Here was the majestic spectacle of a glorious conqueror mightily overthrowing the hostile forces of the devil and nobly bearing the trophy of his victory. On the shoulders of his invincible patience he carried the sign of salvation for all the kingdoms of the earth to worship, as if on that day he would strengthen all his future disciples by the symbol of his work and say to them, "Anyone who does not take up his cross and follow me is not worthy of me." *Sermon 8.4.*

CLOSING PRAYER

O God of love, Who has given a new commandment through your only begotten Son, that we should love one another, even as you loved us, the unworthy and the wandering, and gave your beloved Son for our life and salvation; we pray, Lord, give to us, your servants, in all time of our life on the earth, a mind forgetful of past ill-will, a pure conscience and sincere thoughts, and a heart to love our brothers; for the sake of Jesus Christ, your Son, our Lord and only Savior. Amen. *Coptic Liturgy of St. Cyril*

FURTHER READING: Psalm 22; 40; 54; 95

SATURDAY

✝

"All we like sheep have gone astray; we have turned every one to his own way; and the Lord has laid on him the iniquity of us all." (Isaiah 53:6 BCP)

CONFESSION: See page 11.

SCRIPTURE READING: John 20:10-18

[10]Then the disciples went back to their homes.

[11]But Mary stood weeping outside the tomb, and as she wept she stooped to look into the tomb; [12]and she saw two angels in white, sitting where the body of Jesus had lain, one at the head and one at the feet. [13]They said to her, "Woman, why are you weeping?" She said to them, "Because they have taken away my Lord, and I do not know where they have laid him." [14]Saying this, she turned round and saw Jesus standing, but she did not know that it was Jesus. [15]Jesus said to her, "Woman, why are you weeping? Whom do you

seek?" Supposing him to be the gardener, she said to him, "Sir, if you have carried him away, tell me where you have laid him, and I will take him away." [16]Jesus said to her, "Mary." She turned and said to him in Hebrew, "Rabboni!" (which means Teacher). [17]Jesus said to her, "Do not hold me, for I have not yet ascended to the Father; but go to my brethren and say to them, I am ascending to my Father and your Father, to my God and your God." [18]Mary Magdalene went and said to the disciples, "I have seen the Lord"; and she told them that he had said these things to her.

REFLECTIONS FROM THE CHURCH FATHERS

Our Tears Wiped Away Too, GREGORY THE GREAT. The very declarations of Scripture that excite our tears of love wipe away those very tears by promising us the sight of our Redeemer again. *Forty Gospel Homilies 25.*

Formerly Estranged, We Become Children, GREGORY OF NYSSA. Now that the words addressed to Mary are not applicable to the Godhead of the Only Begotten, one may learn from the intention with which they were uttered. For he who humbled himself to a level with human littleness is the one who spoke these words. . . . He from whom we were formerly alienated by our revolt has become our Father and our God. Accordingly in the passage cited above the Lord brings the good news of this benefit. And the words are not a proof of the degradation of the Son but the good news of our reconciliation to God. For that which has taken place in Christ's humanity is a common boon bestowed on humankind generally. For as when we see in him the weight of the body that naturally gravitates to earth ascending through the air into the heavens, we believe according to the words of the apostle that we also "shall be caught up in the clouds to meet the Lord in the air." Even so, when we hear that the true God and Father has become the God and Father of our Firstfruits, we no longer doubt that the same God has become our God and Father too, inasmuch as we have learned that we shall come to the same place where Christ has entered for us as our forerunner. *Against Eunomius 12.1.*

CLOSING PRAYER

O God, who by your only-begotten Son has overcome death and opened to us the gate of everlasting life; grant us, we implore you, that we who celebrate the solemnities of our Lord's Resurrection, may by the renewing of your Spirit arise from the death of the soul; through the same Jesus Christ our Lord. *Gelasian Sacramentary*

FURTHER READING: Psalm 27; 88; 95

ALLELUIA!

CHRIST IS RISEN.

NOTES

CLOSING PRAYER CITATIONS

Week 1

Sunday—Gregorian Sacramentary, *A Chain of Prayer Across the Ages,* arranged by Selina Fitzherbert Fox (New York: E. P. Dutton, 1943), p. 35.

Monday—Gelasian Sacramentary, *A Chain of Prayer Across the Ages,* arranged by Selina Fitzherbert Fox (New York: E. P. Dutton, 1943), p. 154.

Tuesday—Attributed to St. Benedict, *The Westminster Collection of Christian Prayers*, compiled by Dorothy M. Stewart (Louisville: Westminster John Knox Press, 2002), p. 369.

Wednesday—Gelasian Sacramentary, *A Chain of Prayer Across the Ages,* arranged by Selina Fitzherbert Fox (New York: E. P. Dutton, 1943), p. 176.

Thursday—Irenaeus of Lyons, *The Westminster Collection of Christian Prayers*, compiled by Dorothy M. Stewart (Louisville: Westminster John Knox Press, 2002), p. 98.

Friday—Boniface, *The Westminster Collection of Christian Prayers*, compiled by Dorothy M. Stewart (Louisville: Westminster John Knox Press, 2002), p. 131.

Saturday—Augustine, *The Westminster Collection of Christian Prayers*, compiled by Dorothy M. Stewart (Louisville: Westminster John Knox Press, 2002), p. 162.

Week 2

Sunday—Columbanus, *The Westminster Collection of Christian Prayers*, compiled by Dorothy M. Stewart (Louisville: Westminster John Knox Press, 2002), p. 187.

Monday—Ambrose, *Readings for the Daily Office from the Early Church*, compiled by J. Robert Wright (New York: The Church Hymnal Corporation, 1991), p. 181.

Tuesday—Gelasian Sacramentary, *A Chain of Prayer Across the Ages*, arranged by Selina Fitzherbert Fox (New York: E. P. Dutton, 1943), p. 66.

Wednesday—Clement of Rome, *The Westminster Collection of Christian Prayers*, compiled by Dorothy M. Stewart (Louisville: Westminster John Knox Press, 2002), p. 346.

Thursday—Leonine Sacramentary, *A Chain of Prayer Across the Ages*, arranged by Selina Fitzherbert Fox (New York: E. P. Dutton, 1943), p. 41.

Friday—Origen, *The Westminster Collection of Christian Prayers*, compiled by Dorothy M. Stewart (Louisville: Westminster John Knox Press, 2002), p. 16.

Saturday—Leonine Sacramentary, *The Westminster Collection of Christian Prayers*, compiled by Dorothy M. Stewart (Louisville: Westminster John Knox Press, 2002), p. 164.

Week 3

Sunday—Gelasian Sacramentary, *2000 Years of Prayer*, compiled by Michael Counsell (Harrisburg: Morehouse Publishing, 1999), p. 100.

Monday—Gregory of Nazianzus, *The Westminster Collection of Christian Prayers*, compiled by Dorothy M. Stewart (Louisville: Westminster John Knox Press, 2002), p. 280.

Tuesday—Jerome, *The Westminster Collection of Christian Prayers*, compiled by Dorothy M. Stewart (Louisville: Westminster John Knox Press, 2002), p. 335.

Wednesday—Ephrem the Syrian, *2000 Years of Prayer*, compiled by Michael Counsell (Harrisburg: Morehouse Publishing, 1999), p. 59.

Thursday—Gelasian Sacramentary, *Prayers for Public Worship*, compiled and edited by James Ferguson (New York: Harper & Brothers

Publishers, 1958), p. 54.

Friday—Cyprian, *Prayers for Public Worship,* compiled and edited by James Ferguson (New York: Harper & Brothers, 1958), p. 55.

Saturday—Gelasian Sacramentary, *A Chain of Prayer Across the Ages,* arranged by Selina Fitzherbert Fox (New York: E. P. Dutton, 1943), p. 293.

Week 4

Sunday—Polycarp, *The Westminster Collection of Christian Prayers,* compiled by Dorothy M. Stewart (Louisville: Westminster John Knox Press, 2002), p. 33.

Monday—The Venerable Bede, *The Westminster Collection of Christian Prayers,* compiled by Dorothy M. Stewart (Louisville: Westminster John Knox Press, 2002), p. 57.

Tuesday—Jerome, *2000 Years of Prayer,* compiled by Michael Counsell (Harrisburg: Morehouse Publishing, 1999), p. 29.

Wednesday—From the Liturgy of St. Basil the Great, *2000 Years of Prayer,* compiled by Michael Counsell (Harrisburg: Morehouse Publishing, 1999), pp. 47-48.

Thursday—Gallican Sacramentary, *A Chain of Prayer Across the Ages,* arranged by Selina Fitzherbert Fox (New York: E. P. Dutton, 1943), p. 32.

Friday—Augustine, *The Westminster Collection of Christian Prayers,* compiled by Dorothy M. Stewart (Louisville: Westminster John Knox Press, 2002), p. 308.

Saturday—Augustine, *The Westminster Collection of Christian Prayers,* compiled by Dorothy M. Stewart (Louisville: Westminster John Knox Press, 2002), p. 273.

Week 5

Sunday—Gelasian Sacramentary, *2000 Years of Prayer,* compiled by Michael Counsell (Harrisburg: Morehouse Publishing, 1999), p. 99.

Monday—Leonine Sacramentary, *2000 Years of Prayer*, compiled by Michael Counsell (Harrisburg: Morehouse Publishing, 1999), p. 108.

Tuesday—Liturgy of St. Mark, *A Chain of Prayer Across the Ages*, arranged by Selina Fitzherbert Fox (New York: E. P. Dutton, 1943), p. 71.

Wednesday—Ephraem of Syria, *The Westminster Collection of Christian Prayers*, compiled by Dorothy M. Stewart (Louisville: Westminster John Knox Press, 2002), p. 249.

Thursday—Synesius, *The Macmillan Book of Earliest Christian Hymns*, edited by F. Forrester Church and Terrence J. Mulry (New York: Macmillan, 1988), p. 165.

Friday—Cyprian of Carthage, *2000 Years of Prayer*, compiled by Michael Counsell (Harrisburg: Morehouse Publishing, 1999), p. 17.

Saturday—Gelasian Sacramentary, *A Chain of Prayer Across the Ages*, arranged by Selina Fitzherbert Fox (New York: E. P. Dutton, 1943), p. 155.

Week 6

Sunday—St. Patrick, *The Westminster Collection of Christian Prayers*, compiled by Dorothy M. Stewart (Louisville: Westminster John Knox Press, 2002), p. 137.

Monday—Gregorian Sacramentary, *2000 Years of Prayer*, compiled by Michael Counsell (Harrisburg: Morehouse Publishing, 1999), p. 103.

Tuesday—Leo the Great, *Readings for the Daily Office from the Early Church*, compiled by J. Robert Wright (New York: The Church Hymnal Corporation, 1991), p. 130.

Wednesday—Columbanus, *The Westminster Collection of Christian Prayers*, compiled by Dorothy M. Stewart (Louisville: Westminster John Knox Press, 2002), p. 199.

Thursday—Gelasian Sacramentary, *2000 Years of Prayer*, compiled by Michael Counsell (Harrisburg: Morehouse Publishing, 1999), p. 100.

Friday—Coptic Liturgy of St. Cyril, *A Chain of Prayer Across the Ages*, arranged by Selina Fitzherbert Fox (New York: E. P. Dutton, 1943), p. 48.

Saturday—Gelasian Sacramentary, *Ancient Collects and Other Prayers,* compiled by William Bright (Oxford: James Parker, 1908), p. 54.

THE ANCIENT CHRISTIAN COMMENTARY ON SCRIPTURE
is a twenty-nine-volume series offering contemporary readers the opportunity
to study for themselves the key writings of the early church fathers. Each portion of the commentary allows the living voices of the church in its formative
centuries to speak as they engage in the sacred pages of Scripture.

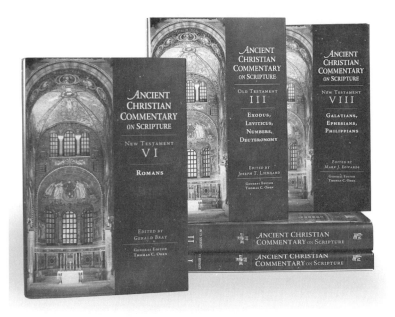

Also available

ANCIENT CHRISTIAN COMMENTARY ON SCRIPTURE

CD-ROM Complete Set

www.ivpress.com/accs